NEW CONSTELLATIONS

BOOKS BY THOMAS M. DISCH

FICTION

The Genocides (1965)
Echo Round His Bones (1966)
Black Alice *(in collaboration with John Sladek)* (1968)
Camp Concentration (1969)
Fun with Your New Head *(Short Stories)* (1970)
334 (1972)
Getting into Death *(Short Stories)* (1976)

POETRY

The Right Way to Figure Plumbing (1972)

ANTHOLOGIES

The Ruins of Earth (1971)
Bad Moon Rising (1973)
The New Improved Sun (1975)

NEW CONSTELLATIONS

AN ANTHOLOGY OF TOMORROW'S MYTHOLOGIES

EDITED BY
THOMAS M. DISCH
& CHARLES NAYLOR

HARPER & ROW, PUBLISHERS
New York, Hagerstown,
San Francisco,
London

FIRST EDITION

Designed by Dorothy Schmiderer

Library of Congress Cataloging in Publication Data

Main entry under title:
New constellations.
    CONTENTS: Diefendorf, D. Fables.—Wolfe, G. Three
fingers.—Kearns, W. The rape of 0000000. [etc.]
    1. Fantastic fiction, American. I. Disch, Thomas M.
II. Naylor, Charles.
PZ1.N426   [PS648.F3]   813'.0876   76-9205
ISBN 0-06-011036-8

76 77 78 79 80 10 9 8 7 6 5 4 3 2 1

For Robert Levy

CONTENTS

INTRODUCTION: MYTHOLOGY AND SCIENCE FICTION

The sun, under which there is nothing new, also rises, and what has happened will happen again, tomorrow and tomorrow and tomorrow. This doctrine, though sanctioned by many authorities, has never found much favor among those whose trade is Novelty—gallery owners, fashion photographers, messiahs, and science-fiction writers.

It can be argued that there are, in fact, new things under the sun nowadays—Concorde jets, Kellogg's Pop-Tarts, sun lamps, the *Tomorrow* show with Tom Snyder, and much else besides, some good, some bad, and all pouring with indiscriminate abundance from the cornucopia of technology.

What hasn't changed (so far) is the nature of the darkly wise being who must confront both old and new and make some sense of them. The forms of that sense are the structures of mythology, the forever-bifurcating, often rickety architectures that support every conceivable (human) meaning.

Myths are everywhere—in every morsel of food, decorating banks and birdhouses, tingeing the blandest discourse with dire resonances, making the mildest encounter a drama. Don't take my word for it: read Freud, or Levi Strauss, or Barthes. In this very broad sense mythology embraces the whole realm of the cultivated and the civilized, everything shaped by the hand and mind of men, which, for most of us, includes everything in sight. Indeed, even where the hand can't reach, the all-conquering imagination extends its empery, staking a claim on the stars by the simple act of connecting the dots and naming the figures formed by the lines: Orion, Cassiopeia, Hercules, Draco.

Myths are everywhere, but especially in literature. Reduce

whatever tale to its atomic components and you'll find those
eternal champions and heroes of a thousand farces, Mr. and Ms.
Mythos. There they are, skulking in the background of even the
likeliest story, disguised as people with next-door names—
Steven, Edward, Anna, Emma—but recognizable for all that as
Adam, Oedipus, Ishtar, or Snow White. It is not the ingenuity
of critics that accomplishes this but simple human nature. We
are a species, alike not only in the morphology of the flesh but
as well in that of the spirit—and limited in both. Limited, too,
in the relations we can form with others. People arrange themselves in pairs, in eternal triangles, in square dances, and so on,
up to about twelve. Thirteen at table is unlucky; fourteen anywhere is a mob (or, if they're *our* mob, a tribe). Like the Sun
Himself, we are prisoners of plane geometry, and the geome-
ters who have described and defined the configurations we are
capable of forming are the makers, and remakers, of our myths.

Myths are everywhere in literature, but especially in science
fiction, in which category I would (for present purposes) include
all distinctively modern forms of fantasy from Tolkien to
Borges. The reasons for this aren't far to seek. Myths aim at
maximizing meaning, at compressing truth to the highest density that the mind can assimilate without the need of, as it were,
cooking. (Extending that metaphor, natural philosophy—science—would represent truth in a less immediately ingestible
form—dry lentils, so to speak.) To attain such compression
myths make free use of the resources of the unconscious mind,
that alternate world where magic still works and metamorphoses are an everyday occurrence. Science fiction presumably
abjures magic but only—like Giordano Bruno, Uri Geller, and
other canny charlatans—in order to escape the Inquisition. In
fact, sf has been trafficking in magic and mythology since first
it came into existence. Mary Shelley's *Frankenstein* is subtitled
"A Modern Prometheus," and the horror-show monsters whose
image continues to be emblematic of the genre are provably
the descendants of "Gorgons and Hydras, and Chimaeras dire."
There is scarcely a theme in sf for which a classic parallel cannot
be found: try it.

As mythmakers, science-fiction writers have a double task,
the first aspect of which is to make humanly relevant—literally,
to humanize—the formidable landscapes of the atomic era. We

must trace in the murky sky the outlines of such new constellations as the Telephone, the Helicopter, the Eight Pistons, the Neurosurgeon, the Cryotron. Often enough, in looking about the heavens for a place to install one of these latter-day figures, the mythmaker discovers that the new figure corresponds very neatly with one already there. The Motorcyclist, for instance, is congruent at almost all points with the Centaur, and no pantheon has ever existed without a great-bosomed, cherry-lipped Marilyn who promises every delight to her devotees. But matching old and new isn't always this easy. Consider the Rocket Ship. Surely it represents something more than a cross between Pegasus and the *Argo*. What distinguishes the Rocket Ship is that (1) it is mechanically powered and that (2) its great speed carries it out of ordinary space into hyperspace, a realm of indefinable transcendence. My theory is that the contemporary human experience that the myth of the Rocket Ship apotheosizes is that of driving, or riding in, an automobile. We may deplore the use of cars as a means of self-realization and of public highways as roads to ecstasy, but only driver-training instructors would deny that this is what cars are all about. And, by extension, the Rocket Ship. The '20s and '30s, when driving was still a relative novelty, were also the heyday of the archetypal—and, in their way, insurpassable—power fantasies of E. E. Smith and other, lesser bards of the Model T. Among adolescents and in countries such as Italy where car ownership confers the same ego satisfaction as surviving a rite of passage, the Rocket Ship remains the most venerated of sf icons—and not because it embodies a future possibility but because it interprets a common experience.

The second task of sf writers as mythmakers is simply the custodial work of keeping the inherited body of myths alive. Every myth is the creation, originally, of a poet, and it remains a vital presence in our culture only so long as it speaks to us with the living breath of living art; so long, that is, as it continues to be twice-told. Everyone pitches in—from Mesopotamian parents recounting the story of Gilgamesh to scholars translating that story into modern languages. Even Homer, probably, felt the anxiety of influence; by Ovid's time *all* stories were old stories. The names might be changed, the scenery altered, but the basic patterns were as fixed and finite as shoemakers' lasts.

This is why Kipling can maintain that "there are nine and sixty ways of constructing tribal lays, and—ever—single—one—of—them—is—right!"

Science-fiction writers do not have a unique responsibility toward preserving the body of inherited myth. It is a task that we share with poets, painters, playwrights, choreographers, composers, and commentators of every description. I offer the following catalogue not so much as an Extra-Credit Reading List (though they will all get you points) but to suggest the variety, range, and universality of the undertaking. Among works that conscientiously retell discrete myths from beginning to end are T. H. White's *The Once and Future King,* Joyce's *Ulysses,* Richard Adams' *Watership Down,* Cynthia Ozick's *The Pagan Rabbi,* Mary Renault's *The King Must Die,* Mann's *Joseph and His Brothers,* any number of plays by Yeats, Eliot, O'Neill, Gide, Giraudoux, Anouilh, and Sartre; operas by Bartók, Schoenberg, Strauss, and Stravinsky. Additionally, there are writers who, instead of retelling one specific tale, retrace the underlying structures of mythology as these have been systematized by scholars like the Grimm brothers, Frazer, Graves, and Joseph Campbell. Notable among such "synthetic legends" have been Goethe's *"Marchen"* (perhaps the first artificial folk tale), Koch's *Ko,* Barth's *Giles Goat-Boy,* Hofmannsthal's libretto for *Die Frau ohne Schatten,* and Naomi Mitchison's *The Corn King and the Spring Queen.*

Only in the last ten or fifteen years have science-fiction writers shown much interest in the preservative, as against the interpretive, side of mythmaking. The most obvious reason is that writers for the early pulps were not notable for literary sophistication. Van Vogt's stories, at their best, have some of the charm of fairy tales, but I doubt that this was ever his aim. Similarly, the standard space opera often follows a pattern strikingly similar to that which Joseph Campbell describes in *The Hero of a Thousand Faces,* but again I would submit that the likeness was inadvertent. (Though not, of course, accidental: archetypes are hard to avoid once you've set out to tell a story.)

The writers of the '50s, such as Blish, Knight, or Bester, though themselves men of undoubted literary culture, were obliged to write for a naïve audience for whom almost any story was mind-blowing. The shades of irony or degrees of finesse that may distinguish one revision of a familiar story from the next are lost on readers for whom just the idea sets their sense of wonder to tingling.

What changed in the early '60s wasn't the nature of sf writers but of their audience. Simply, it had grown up. Not all readers, of course. There were still, there are still, and there will always be those for whom sf represents their first trip into the realms of gold. But now side by side with these are readers who can be counted on to know more about the life of the mind than can be discovered in the works of Edgar Rice Burroughs and Charles Fort; who have the knack of reading books in pretty much the spirit they were written.

The point, for instance, of Michael Moorcock's *Behold the Man* isn't that, gee whiz, a Time Traveler questing for the historical Jesus is involved in a case of mistaken identities. The point isn't What Happens Next because the reader is assumed to be able to foresee that. The point is, rather, how seamlessly the modern (ironic) version of the myth can be made to overlay the gospel (and so, inevitable) version. To a large degree, therefore, the point is the author's wit, his grace, and his depth. In a word, style.

Style, not in the niggling sense of being able on demand to use the subjunctive and to come up with metaphors, similes and stuff like that. Style, rather, in the exclamatory Astaire-and-Rogers sense of (in the words of Webster's) "Overall excellence, skill, or grace in performance, manner, or appearance."

As to the particular twice-told tales that have been chosen for this anthology, most are based on specific myths, Bible stories, and fairy tales. A few, notably Robert Sheckley's magnificent novella, "In a Land of Clear Colors," are synthetic or composite myths.

The epigraphs, except for the lines from Swinburne before Sheckley's story, are the editors' contribution.

What is the secret of the timeless vision? From what profundity of the mind does it derive? Why is mythology everywhere the same, beneath its varieties of costume? And what does it teach?

Today many sciences are contributing to the analysis of the riddle. Archaeologists are probing the ruins of Iraq, Honan, Crete, and Yucatan. Ethnologists are questioning the Ostiaks of the river Ob, the Boobies of Fernando Po.

—Joseph Campbell,
The Hero with a Thousand Faces

FABLES

BY DAVID DIEFENDORF

THE FROG PRINCE

Once upon a time, five years ago to be exact, I met a prince who lived in a castle in a fairy kingdom. He looked sad. We had dinner together and he told me about his strange problem.

"It's no secret," he said, "that there are all kinds of curses going around in Fairyland. But alas, mine is among the more awkward. What happens is that on occasion I turn into an unsightly frog. It seems to happen when I feel a sudden lapse of self-esteem. I guess you could compare it to stammering, only this is more bizarre and troublesome, as you might imagine. It's got me pretty depressed."

The prince looked depressed. His eyes were red and watery. "Has this frog business been going on long?" I asked.

"It first happened when I was ten," he said. "When I built a shoddy tree house and my father the king called me Dumbkin. I don't think he was trying to be mean, but it struck me that way at the time and in a matter of seconds I had changed from a little boy to a homely amphibian. I stayed that way for two days. A few years later, when I asked a damsel to the royal prom and she said, 'Fat chance,' it happened again. It got more and more frequent. It was especially embarrassing when it happened on job interviews, or in the presence of damsels I was trying to impress."

"How is it these days?" I asked.

"Worse than ever," he said. "It seems to happen at the slightest provocation. When we moved to the new castle a few years ago, a time of minor stress, it happened in front of the servants as I was unpacking. Lately, though, anything can touch it off. If I have a bad night I wake up a slimy frog."

"What exactly happens? Do you just turn into a little frog?"

"No, a big frog. My height and weight stay the same, and I can still walk upright on two legs, but everything else is frog. I can still think, but not as clearly, and speak, but in a barely intelligible baritone. And I tend to snap my jaws at passing insects. All in all, it's not so painful, just humiliating."

"Have you seen a doctor?" I asked.

"Of course. I went to a dermatologist but he told me the problem was psychosomatic and referred me to a psychiatrist. I went to the psychiatrist and he told me the problem was medical. When I told him I'd already been to a dermatologist he said, 'Well, in that case I guess you'll just have to live with it.'"

I regretted leaving the Frog Prince in such a state of turmoil, but I could offer no advice and I had to be moving on to the next kingdom. I wished him luck and said farewell.

Only last month I found myself in the Frog Prince's kingdom for the second time and paid him a visit. He seemed to be in good spirits. "You seem to be in good spirits," I said.

"Quite," he said. "In the years you've been away a few things have changed. My father the king retired early and passed the throne on to me. Since I've been king my self-esteem has improved remarkably, hence I metamorphose less. Also, I had the good fortune to meet and marry a beautiful princess from another kingdom. We met through a service that pairs anomalous royalty. She has a problem similar to mine. When overconfident, she turns into an unruly palomino mare."

"Doesn't that add to your problems?" I asked.

"Not at all. We complement each other. When I'm a frog and she's a horse I climb on her back and we gallop together through the fields and forests of our sublime kingdom. In the process, she feels grotesque and I feel heroic. I bring her down a bit and she brings me up a bit until we are back to normal. We sort of neutralize each other."

"Splendid," I said. The prince looked rosy-cheeked as he poured me another glass of blackberry brandy. "Splendid," he affirmed.

The Frog Prince and his bride lived happily ever after.

MICKEY MOUSE

I was assigned to interview Mickey Mouse. When he walked into the room I noticed he was much taller than I remembered him to be. He said, "I don't sing or dance anymore. I gave up all that silliness a long time ago." He went on to explain that lately he's been interested in literature, especially the work of George Eliot, and that Pluto's untimely death was responsible for his much publicized conversion to Catholicism. He wanted to dispel some popular myths, also. First of all, he said, Minnie Mouse never existed. She was just a fictional character invented by Disney's staff. He said people in the inner circle used to kid him about it all the time. Secondly, he said, he received no formal education whatsoever and for many years was not even able to talk. "This will come as a great surprise to most Americans," he said.

Further along in the interview he discussed a more controversial issue. "I was never interested in other mice," he said. "Not in their problems, not in their pride as a species, not in their politics, because I never considered myself one of them. I never truly identified with my fellow mice." He said he'd been criticized for that, but never took it seriously. "I don't even look like a mouse," he said.

He went on to discuss sexuality. "Most of what you've heard about that part of my life is true," he said. "I don't have any sex to speak of. People think it's a joke. They don't laugh in my face, but I can tell what they're thinking. They point, they whisper, but I don't care anymore. I'm forty-seven now, and I'm no baby. I can handle my own affairs. If I can't cope I just bow out for a while, cool off for a while, take a powder."

Mickey said he felt like taking a powder. On his way out the door he extended his glove to me and we shook hands. " 'Bye now," he said, giving me a maturer, faintly bitterer version of the grin that had endeared him to millions. *"Au revoir, rongeur,"* I said. "And give my best to Minnie."

. . . It was one thing to eat one from time to time—that was only natural: kept them from overpopulating, maybe starving to death, come winter—but it was another thing to scare them, give them heart attacks, fill their nights with nightmares, just for sport.

—John Gardner, *Grendel*

THREE FINGERS

BY GENE WOLFE

"Look at them. Look at these."

"Wha . . . ?" The little boy stretched out a hand, thrusting his chubby arm through the diamond mesh of the playground fence.

"Only a dime," Michael said.

"I don't have a dime."

"They're real. Tell your friends. I'll be back next week." He took the cigar box from under his arm and began to replace the bright plastic figures on the cotton inside. "I've got Pinocchio and Geppetto and Stromboli. Did you ever try to *buy* Stromboli?"

"I gotta go back now."

Michael watched the little boy march back to school, then turned away. There was a store, a store he hadn't tried to sell yet, way out on 44th. He pulled up the collar of his pea jacket and edged out into the street to hitch a ride. The pea jacket was a size "S," but Michael was thin and looked tall. The wind whipped his long hair around his face.

He thought: *No black cars,* looking behind him for a doorway or an alley in case one should come. *They mostly use those big black ones with four doors and maybe shades on the windows. Those are the MM cars.* A hearse turned the corner and he threw himself flat and rolled under a parked truck. They hadn't expected him to do that and didn't see him.

He wiggled out and dusted himself off and a bottle-green Pontiac driven by a stout woman with a mink stole picked him up. She said, "I have two sons at Antioch; they're both doing very well. Are you in college? Where are you going?"

"Up on Forty-fourth Street."

"Fine. I'm going right past there." She smiled.

"There's this store there that sells old books and knickknacks. I mean, like, if you want the nineteen forty-three Captain Midnight Secret Decoder they've probably got it. Want to see what I'm going to sell them?" Michael opened his cigar box and, when the Pontiac stopped for a light, held it up so the woman could see the contents.

"What are those?" She reached out plump, diamonded fingers. "Why, it's Snow White. I haven't seen Snow White for years."

"These were cast in nineteen thirty-five, two years before the movie was released. Only for collectors. Look at the detail on them."

"I didn't know they had plastic way back then." The woman's voice was interested and friendly.

"It's celluloid. They don't look old because they're mint specimens. They've been kept in a box, just like this, away from sunlight and everything, all this time. I got some at home that look older, but I usually take these when I'm going to try to sell to kids because the kids like them new. And look here." He lifted the cotton and pulled a sheaf of glossy photographs from under it. "You'll dig these. Dedicated photographs—not just autographed you understand, dedicated—of Tommy Kirk and Annette. See, where they signed it's not just reproduced with the picture when they reprinted it. It's signed on *this* copy with a real pen. And there's something written underneath to a particular person. That's Tommy Kirk you're looking at. He was a lot younger then."

"They're beautiful," the woman said. She was keeping one eye on her driving.

"He really wrote it himself. Now look here. Here's a photostat of an authenticated letter of his. See how he makes his *y*'s? See how the *t*'s are? Now look at this dedication." Michael's knee kept slipping through a tear in his blue jeans as he spoke, and all his gestures were interrupted by the desertions of his left hand, which made quick trips to draw the torn cloth together. He straightened the leg as much as he could, putting his foot high up on the firewall.

"It's very nice," the woman said. "It makes me think of the time when my boys were smaller."

"Well, say your name is Clarice, right? So . . ." Michael

shuffled rapidly through the photographs. "So you could have a picture on your dresser that says, 'To Clarice, my most beautiful and dearly beloved fan. Tommy Kirk.' That's cool, huh?"

"My name's June. Do you have one that says June?"

"No, but I could get you one. Give me your address and I would bring it around."

"I think I'll just take Snow White. How much is Snow White?"

Michael reflected. The woman looked as if she might pay a dollar, and with a dollar . . . "Eighty-five cents," he said. "I'm sorry it's so much, but, you know, inflation."

"My husband says the same thing," June said, rummaging in her purse.

She let him out at the corner of 44th, but the store was closed. A sign on the door read: "Closed due to illness of proprietor." Michael rattled the knob, but the door was locked.

He thumbed for nearly an hour before a married couple named Harley and Amaryllis gave him a ride back on their Triumph bike. He bounced along behind Amaryllis; but there was too much noise for him to sell her anything, and the MM almost got him within a block of the place where he lived.

He was going to go into the White Castle for a bowl of chili when he saw the ears of the man at the counter. Not human ears. Soft ears, ears that hung straight down like the ears of a beagle puppy, but smaller. He started to run, but that would tip them off; they would expect that. He crossed the street and sat at the soda fountain, where he could watch the man in the White Castle. *Keep them under surveillance,* he thought, *that's tough. If you know where they are you can be where they're not looking.*

Across the street in the White Castle the man with the soft ears sat hunched over his cheeseburger. Michael wanted to say to the white-capped, white-coated boy behind the marble counter, *Hey, man, look over across the street with the black coat and the rolled-down white gloves, with the soft ears. He's from the Mickey Mafia, man, and he's after me. I steal their stuff all the time, and they don't like that.* But the poor goop probably didn't even know what the MM *was,* and instead Michael took out his jap pen and did Tommy Kirk's signature perfectly on the countertop, then put Annette's under it and drew a heart around them. That made him think of a shield, so he gave the heart Ben Ali Gator and Hyacinth Hippo for supporters and a sailor cap with a ribbon for a crest. Then the boy who fixed the sodas made him leave.

It was cold outside and he tried to sell one of Annette's pictures and a statuette of Pinocchio without success. The woman who ran the place where he lived said, "Did you have a nice walk, Mr. Moss?"

"Okay, I guess. Awfully cold. No callers for me?"

"No callers, Mr. Moss."

"You wouldn't let them in if they came, would you? I mean even if they knew my name and said they were friends of mine. You wouldn't let them into my room?"

The woman smiled, smoothing her white dress with her hands, wanting to be busy again. "I wouldn't let them in, Michael."

He went upstairs, his chest tightening all the time as the fear built up in him. When he had found his key he waited outside the door, not wanting to open it for fear he would find everything gone.

Then he did, and it was okay. If they had come they would have wrecked everything, but his injection molding machine—the smallest size built, but it still dwarfed the room—stood as he had left it. His molds, carved from aluminum with the Dremel Moto-Tool and finished after long hours of work with the needle files, were heaped beside it. Nearby were the cans of multicolored polyethylene granules, one (yellow for dancing mushrooms) spilled on the floor—but he had done that himself. He hung up his coat and warmed his fingers under his arms.

What now? A wristwatch? They sold best of all, and he could use the money. He picked up one of the inexpensive watches he bought to convert and looked it over, then took down his cap, the cap that had begun it all, from its peg of honor over his bed. The round ears he had cut from black felt were soft and floppy now, but they reminded him of home. The others had had them and he had not wanted to wait. He had made his own, sewing the ears—with a little help from his mother—to an old skull cap of his father's. He brushed his hair back with his hand and set the cap firmly on his head.

Then as though that had been what they were waiting for they came out.

Captain Hook, with his cruel steel hand and the long curls down to his shoulders, came out of the lavatory. His "Captain Hook" face was a latex Halloween mask, but Michael had not made it.

The Big Bad Wolf came from the closet. His rubber mask had a grotesquely upturned snout, his rubber eyes a sly glint (with the holes for real eyes two dark dots below them), and his rubber teeth were huge. He wore a red flannel shirt and dirty overalls with a broken strap.

And the Wicked Queen came from the dark corner where his books were piled. Her face was hard and cold, and her black robe swept the floor. A poisoned dagger hung at her waist on a thin gold chain.

"All right," Michael said, "I guess it's all over."

"It is indeed," said Captain Hook.

"I guess I don't get a last request."

"No," Captain Hook said, "you do not." He was opening a package, tearing away the wrapping paper with his shining claw. "We have a certain ceremony to observe, a ritual of execution, but last requests are not included."

"I was going to ask you to take off your masks."

"And why," inquired the Wicked Queen, "were you going to ask that?"

"Because I've worked with all of you so long that I think I know who you are really, and I'd like to see if I'm right."

Captain Hook laughed. "And who am I?"

"Blackbeard and Captain Kidd and Sir Henry Morgan and Calico Jack and Barbarossa and maybe a little Captain Bligh."

"And me," said the Big Bad Wolf, leering. "Who'm I, huh?"

"You're the wolf of old Europe; the wolf that tore the sentries to bits in front of the Winter Palace at St. Petersburg. The wolf that was killed by the invention of repeating firearms like the great god Pan by the coming of Christ. The wolf people now say never existed, and forget all the stories. The wolf that took the baby pigs from the farmyard at noon and the children when they walked through the forest. You are Baron Isengrim."

"And I," said the Wicked Queen. "If I were to take this mask off who would I be, wise boy?"

"Lucrezia Borgia and Catherine de Medici. Morgan le Fay

and all the great ladies who beat the peasants' children to frighten their own."

"As my colleague told you," said the Wicked Queen, "we have a certain ritual of death. Captain, show him what you have."

Captain Hook held out an open candy box. The cardboard, once highly ornamented, was crumbling with age now, and the bright inks had faded. It held bonbons of a fondant time was turning back to sugar and a cloying perfume. Two red jellybeans rolled loose in the lid.

"We shall kill you with these," the Wicked Queen told Michael. "It is—perhaps you will appreciate this—the most honorable of the means of execution we use. The jellybeans will be thrust up your nostrils; then the bonbons will be stuffed into your throat until you suffocate of surfeit of sweetness. But first we will grant your last request."

She raised her arms as though invoking some high power. "Mirror, mirror, on the wall, who is underneath it all?"

The Big Bad Wolf drew off his mask, pulled off his flannel shirt, stepped out of his overalls, and was a paunchy man in a business suit. Captain Hook set the bonbons on a table, dropped his hook, peeled off his mask and wig, and was a paunchy man in a business suit. The Wicked Queen unhooked the mask from behind her ears, slid out of her black robe, and was a paunchy woman in a tailored suit. Before Michael could resist, the man who had been Captain Hook and the man who had been the Big Bad Wolf had seized him by the arms and the woman who had been the Wicked Queen was pushing the red jellybeans into his nose. He tried to hold his mouth shut, but she pried his jaws open and forced in a yellow bonbon.

He tried to swallow it before she could get in another and found that it had become a red jellybean too and went down easily.

"What is it?" said the man who had been Captain Hook.

"Synthetic para-reserpine," said the woman. "I've had good luck with it on him." She touched Michael's face with a white/red rubber-gloved hand that had four/three fingers.

. . . At this match (as after will appeare)
Was neyther Juno, President of marriage wont to be,
Nor Hymen, no nor any one of all the graces three.
The Furies snatching Tapers up that on some Herce did stande
Did light them, and before the Bride did beare them in their hande.
The Furies made the Bridegroomes bed. And on the house did rucke
A cursed Owle the messenger of yll successe and lucke.
And all the night time while that they were lying in their beds,
She sate upon the bedsteds top right over both their heds.
Such handsell Progne had the day that Tereus did hir wed.
Such handsell had they when that she was brought of childe abed.

—Golding's *Ovid*

THE RAPE OF OOOOOOO

BY WINN KEARNS

Rocketplanes once droned above the captive planet, zinged a bomb here and there when the target was either a roaming dog or a lone plodder with her bedroll in a shoulder pack. A spaghetti mess of circuitry engirdled the forsaken tower building. Planes carried the grandeur of war, rows of medals, the bugle tap for arousal at dawn, the quickened step of those not dead yet who air-marched toward those who would deaden them. Planes were the well-spoken-of population controllers. Blink the laser beam, snip off the noses, call it the Holy Crusades. Label it mankind with no more sense than to masturbate by tying a string around his projecting sausage-shaped machine, then—with the end of the string tied around a doorknob—open and shut the door.

The planet had lost its name when the computer blew a fuse with the programmer mixed up on his data printouts on planets, and ending with a string of 0000000 for his own.

Grotwahn, whizzer of oratory, thumped guttalk as he stood on a pedestal declaring that he would solve population control. "War disposes of those unfit to be fit," he intoned. "Our planet should enact a statute making it unlawful for the male to abort life by pulling out before he inseminates the female. By doing this, planet 0000000 loses its population. Our laws need to increase population when we have population control by war."

Grotwahn needed an audience even on a desolate landscape. And as chance would have it, there were two of us who had met in the shrubbery near the pedestal. Hortense was eastbound; I was westbound. We decided to rest from our traveling and listen to Grotwahn. Dust of the road was an incisive factor in the decision. Both of us noticed the chips on our fingernails. So, down we sat.

13

"Do you think I should take a potshot at Grotwahn with my rifle?" I asked.

Hortense, who was painting her fingernails, looked up from her brushwork. "No," she said. "We might wait until he gets around to telling us that wars are performed for the protection of women and children who have no wish to fight."

"Women are the servants who supply the war machine with progeny," Grotwahn intoned. His eyebrows beetled at us. "They cook the food to feed the boy who grows to man the planes to bomb. Does a man go to warfare for his own protection? No, fellow citizens of planet 0000000. He protects the women from savagery. He makes the home safe for survival."

"Perhaps we should plug him between the eyes," Hortense muttered.

"So you've changed your mind? You are certainly changeable, Hortense." I held up my fingernails; the chipped appearance was gone. "Maybe we should paint our toenails. It would give us something to do."

"History repeats itself," intoned Grotwahn. "When you read history, you will observe that it has cycles, war with a short space of peace, then war again, peace again, war peace war peace round and around in the circle face of the clock."

"Are you mouthing the past?" Hortense shouted at Grotwahn. "Your circle, instead of a clock, resembles a dog biting its tail."

"Paint your toenails," he intoned harshly. "Women were made to beautify the landscape and become, during intervals of peace, our gracious pastures and meadows with clover growing."

Hortense became impatient with him. "On 0000000, as you well know, the men are killing each other off. They have already—except for a dozen or so. History will wind down and stop cold."

"Right you are," Grotwahn conceded but with a sigh. "I do believe you have a point. Men endeavoring to control population may have a faulty spring. Ping! A snap. Silence. But don't forget the pastures and meadows. They still exist."

"Thank you for the information," Hortense said. She then turned toward me and asked what form I would like to take in the meadow. "We must seed ourselves," she told me and added that she had always fancied herself as a pecan tree.

I, more weepy, decided to be a willow and mourn the men who had passed on through history.

"May I join you ladies?" Grotwahn asked. "For myself, I favor being a toad."

"But what about population control?" I asked.

"To hell with it," he said, and then he shriveled, turned green and warty-skinned.

All was quiet on 0000000 except for now and then a glub-glub in the dark and the whisper of wind on the leaves.

At Cincinnati there is a garden where the people go to eat ices and to look at roses. For the preservation of the flowers, there is placed at the end of one of the walks a signpost sort of daub, representing a Swiss peasant girl, holding in her hand a scroll, requesting that the roses might not be gathered.

—Mrs. Trollope,
Domestic Manners of the Americans

EARTHBLOSSOM

BY JON FAST

Ruth Schulman was running through the woods the day she found the plant. Her vision was blurred by tears and the dense canopy of leaves overhead cut out the sunlight, but she could see well enough to recognize that the plant was unlike any she had ever seen before.

It was as tall as she was—almost six feet—a deep greenish purple in color and shaped like an elongated pine cone. Wiping her eyes, she began to inspect it more closely.

The leaves grew in overlapping circles of seven, pointed at the top and covered with a fine red tracery. Gingerly she reached out and fingered the edge of one. It felt stiff, like leather. Toward the bottom the leaves became smaller and grew straight out, parallel to the ground. Kneeling, she could see below them a stem, fully two feet wide and also veined in red, the veins as thick as fingers. As she watched they seemed to pulse to a secret rhythm.

Ruth felt no fear, only wonder and a sort of thankfulness for such an interesting distraction.

Smiling, she stood up and addressed the plant:

"You're a great big artichoke, and I *love* artichokes. I'm going back to the hotel for ten pounds of melted butter—then you better watch out!"

Ugly girls have to develop a sense of humor.

It took fifteen minutes to get out of the woods and another ten to cross the eighteen-hole golf course behind Hideaway in the Poconos Hotel. No one was playing the course, Ruth noticed; they were all still at the "Get Acquainted Bloody-Mary-and-Brunch Pool Party." Get acquainted. Some of the sadness came back to her, but she pushed it aside.

It was not her fault; she had tried. The new bathing suit had cost her thirty-two dollars at Saks, the beach robe another thirty. She had starved herself and taken off eleven pounds before leaving New York and had had her hair done by the same hairdresser Kathy went to.

Yet sitting by the pool that morning, she might have been invisible. The handsome young men with their carefully cropped mustaches and sideburns and beefy physiques crowded around Kathy, who lay in the deck chair next to Ruth's like royalty, graciously accepting Bloody Marys and plates of scrambled eggs and sausages. Compliments and invitations.

Ruth thought: we haven't even been here an hour and it's begun. Two more weeks of this, of living in Kathy's shadow, of being ignored. I will leave Tuesday or Wednesday.

She was planning her excuses when she felt the wetness between her shoulders. Her right hand explored the back of her robe; somehow scrambled eggs had become wedged in the space between her and the chair. Her beautiful new robe. It was really more than she could bear. With studied reserve she rose from the deck chair and left the pool; only upon reaching the lee of the hotel did she let the tears flow. Lest anyone should see her, she ran for the protection of the woods beyond the golf course.

Ruth was a bird face, little round eyes and a long sharp nose, perched atop a dinosaur body. Her hips were broad as a battleship. No matter what she did with her hair, it looked like a cheap rayon wig. All this in an age when slimness and nice hair were valued like diamonds.

People tolerated her when she was funny, but since adolescence Ruth had become more and more susceptible to lengthy blue periods of introspection and self-pity. During these times she would eat and read paperback Gothics and historical romances by Georgette Heyer.

The night table held a stack of these, slick, not yet dog-eared, covers depicting beautiful girls with beautiful hair (the one on *The Mystery of Fineholt Manor* reminded her of Kathy) looking beautiful and windblown on the heath. Castles and Tudor mansions loomed behind, one light burning in one high tower window.

Opposite the night table a Van Gogh print hung above a

writing desk that might have been wood but wasn't, provisioned with Hideaway in the Poconos stationery and Hideaway in the Poconos postcards. Oddly, the Poconos were nowhere in sight.

The pamphlet had promised "Two weeks of sun and fun for swinging singles, just a stone's throw from the glorious Poconos," and there had been glossy photographs of a stone cottage with broad eaves and leaded windows, a room with a fireplace and thick rug, two beds covered with patchwork quilts. Like something in a storybook.

But when Ruth and Kathy arrived, they were directed to an austere two-story concrete complex. The management, a baldheaded monkey of a man who unsuccessfully affected youthful dress to keep up with the times, was sorry. The cottage pictured in the pamphlet had been torn down eight years ago to make room for the new building. It was all for the better, the management assured them. The old cottages had been double occupancies; the new complex was single occupancy with friendly connecting baths. That way if one of them (and it was understood that the "one" was Kathy) met a boy who made bells ring, it wouldn't be any inconvenience for the other. The management winked broadly so there could be no misunderstandings about hotel policy.

Ruth was absorbed in *The Mystery of Fineholt Manor* and only gradually became aware of voices in the next room. The door on Kathy's side of the bathroom must have been left open. It was a minute more before she understood they were talking about her. She could hear Kathy's voice, faintly:

". . . and it's not nice to call her that. Her name's Ruthie, Ruthie Schulman."

"But that's who she reminds me of. Honest!" (Ruth recognized the second voice as belonging to a young man she had seen at the pool that morning. He was an excellent diver, an impossible show-off.) "The bride of Frankenstein."

Laughter.

"What's wrong with calling her the bride of Frankenstein?" (Another voice. Ruth didn't know him.)

"Frankenstein might get insulted." (That was the Diver again.)

"Dicky! That's *not* nice."

"How did a fantastic chick like you get mixed up with a monster like her anyway?"

"We have an apartment together. I met her through one of those roommate agencies—Great Mates. And she's not a monster! She's very sensitive and intelligent and . . ."

And kind and has a wonderful personality, Ruth thought, completing the inevitable series. She could imagine them in the next room, Kathy sticking out of her bikini, the two boys being casual and sophisticated. Kathy again:

". . . you know why she left the party? I thought she looked upset."

"Well . . ." (The Diver, chuckling.) "I got kind of curious about what Mrs. Frankenstein looked like under that robe, and I was standing right behind her, so I sort of accidentally dropped some of my scrambled eggs . . ."

Ruth rolled over and shut her eyes.

Ruth passed Kathy in the lobby.

"You're up early," Kathy said. "Have breakfast with me?"

Ruth shook her head. "Maybe if I stay out of the dining room I can lose some weight."

"Good girl," Kathy said maternally and launched into an opera bouffe anecdote about the previous night: two boys, drunk, climbing in her window, tripping on the light cord. Noticing Ruth edging toward the door, she cut it short and asked, with a trace of annoyance, just where she was in such a hurry to get to.

"The woods."

"Dressed like that?" Kathy raised an eyebrow.

"I'm . . ." Ruth hesitated. "I'm going to meet a friend."

Kathy gave her a sly smile—"Don't do anything I wouldn't do"—and, turning on her heels, went to breakfast.

The plant had grown four inches since the day before. The uppermost points of the leaves were no longer touching but had formed a mouth at the very top, perhaps two feet across. Ruth wished that she was tall enough to see down into the opening. It was the first time in her life she'd wanted to be taller.

"So," she said, patting the leaves affectionately, "you're not an artichoke after all. You're a great big bud. And it's lucky for you, 'cause I was planning to have you for lunch." Then, wistfully: "I sure hope you flower soon. I'm only going to be here for two weeks."

People talk to dogs; they talk to babies; society approves. Others even converse with empty air and are tolerated. In light of this, what happened next is not really so strange. Ruth cleared a space of pine needles and pebbles, sat down crosslegged, primly arranging her skirt to cover her knees, and proceeded to spend the better part of the morning telling the plant about her early childhood, unhappy college years, a younger sister whom she disliked, teaching nursery school, which she liked, and all she had overheard the night before from an adjoining room.

"Ruthie? Ruthie, come on. You'll miss all the fun!"

"What?" Ruth asked, lying on the bed, her head propped up on pillows, staring absently at the Van Gogh print on the opposite wall. It was a picture of sunflowers, a ghost of the original.

"Coed karate lessons on the tennis court," Kathy explained impatiently. "They started twenty minutes ago. There's this adorable little Oriental man . . . His name's Phong Wu or something like that . . ."

"I don't think so, Kathy. I'm a little bushed."

"Ruthie!" Kathy put her hands on her hips; her tiny rosebud mouth pouted. "Do you mean that after saving all year for this vacation you're going to spend two weeks in a hotel room mooning around like a sick cow? You won't meet *anyone* this way!" Kathy stamped her foot. "I won't allow it. I simply will not allow it."

Ruth got up and hugged her friend. "You're a dear, Kathy. But you shouldn't worry about me. I've already made a friend."

Earlier, when she had been sitting on the dirt, talking to the plant, her knees had grown stiff and she had lain down on her back, making a pillow from her fingers. So the back of her skirt and blouse were covered with dirt and twigs and pine needles. Kathy noticed this and, remembering their conversation that morning, drew her own conclusions.

"Your friend in the woods?"

Ruth nodded.

"Well, for heaven's sake. Why don't you do things with him

at the hotel? You could go to the karate lessons together. He is a guest here, isn't he? Or is he a local?"

"Um . . . yes, I mean no. He is, but he's very shy." And Ruth added, "You see, he's from Alaska." (She had once known a very shy boy from Alaska.)

Kathy wrinkled her nose, which turned up like a Dutch shoe; then she smiled and tossed up her hands. "Oh, Ruthie, I don't know *what* to do with you!"

That night there was a storm. Ruth lay in bed listening to the thunder, the heavy drops drumming against the roof. Sunflowers exploded in the lightning.

By morning the rain had stopped, but the ground was still wet; her feet sank into the earth. She brushed against branches and they snapped back, catapulting water on her yellow oilcloth slicker. An elephantine canary. Pines and tall elms and maples glistened in the early sunlight and the forest smelled rich, like living things.

Ruth gasped when she saw the plant. It might have been the rain or simply that, when the time is right, plants hurry to bloom. Certain cacti, after years of excruciatingly slow growth, will manufacture the most elaborate flowers without a moment's notice.

The pointed greenish-purple leaves had flattened into a broad bowl easily fourteen feet across and as high as Ruth's waist. In the center, rising like an enormous stamen, was a man of such grace and beauty that for a moment Ruth doubted her sanity. As she stood there dumbfounded, he opened one eye, then the other and smiled at her.

Dicky Bliss would have ascended to heaven, rung by rung, if the ladder had reached that far. There were no lengths he would not have gone to to please his audience. Yet masculine pride dictated indifference, so he kept his head erect, eyes forward. Three steps from the edge of the high diving board, his resolution wavered and he looked down, way down to the left of the pool where he knew Kathy was sitting. Yes, there she was in her fantastic bikini but, damn it, not paying a bit of attention. To hell with her, Dicky decided, and sprang off the board.

Anger had gotten the better of discipline. The third somersault went incomplete, his back slapped the water and came up lobster red. Raising himself over the side of the pool, he hopped to where Kathy was sunning and shook water on her like a dog.

"Stop it!" she squealed, and "You're horrible!"

"I was bringing you back to the living. You missed a nearly perfect triple gainer."

"I was thinking about Ruthie."

"Are you still on that?" Dicky sighed and dropped into the chair next to her.

"You know how sweet and innocent she is. I don't want to see her get hurt."

"Is she on the pill?" Dicky asked.

Kathy waved him away. "That's not what I mean. It's that . . . well . . . the way I see it, here's some man who's happy to *you-know-what* with Ruthie every day in the woods but ashamed to be seen with her in public. It's not fair. He's not fulfilling his part of the bargain."

"The bargain?"

"Yes. If a girl's going to do . . . *that*, then in return she should be dined and danced with and taken places in public."

"Oh."

"And he thinks he can get away with it just because Ruthie's so . . . you know . . ."

"Hideous?"

"Plain. It's just not fair. Listen, Dicky, will you do something for me?"

"Will I!" He knelt by her feet and, twisting the towel around his head like a burnous, vowed in a bad Arab accent, "I will carry you across the desert on my back with only a moist piece of blotting paper for sustenance; I will swim the Amazon . . ."

"Dicky, be serious! You know what tonight is?"

The question was rhetorical. They'd been discussing it all week.

"The Fabulous Fifties Nostalgia Sock Hop."

"Yes. And can you guess who isn't going?"

"Uh . . . King Farouk? Elizabeth Taylor? Okay, sorry. Madam Frankenstein."

"Yes. And it's just *not* fair. Dicky, I want you to follow her to the woods. See who her bashful friend is. Once we know . . ."

"We can blackmail him?"

"We can convince him to escort Ruthie to the Sock Hop. It's the least he can do for her."

Branches raked Ruthie's face. She couldn't push them away because her hands were occupied. Under each arm she carried boxes displaying a jumble of odd-sized circumflexes meant to represent the Poconos Mountains, the insignia of a modish clothes store in town. Dicky followed stealthy in sneakers at twenty feet. At the edge of a small clearing he knelt behind a tree.

A man was waiting, sitting on a rock, doing nothing. He wore only blue jeans. The hair on his chest and head were light gold; his face was like a Greek statue, even the eyes, which might have been chipped from marble. Something about him took Dicky's breath away.

Ruth set down her packages, and, pulling the man to his feet, they kissed. For a long time.

"I bought you clothes for the Sock Hop," Ruth said with excitement. "You'll be beautiful."

"Sock Hop?" the man asked slowly. His voice made Dicky think of wind blowing through trees.

"It's too complicated to explain. Just do what I say, and you'll be fine."

She dressed him in argyles, tan and bone saddle shoes, tight jeans—the ones he was wearing were baggy, loose around the waist; they were Ruth's—and a shirt with a button-down collar.

Ruth bent his arms forward to receive the shirt; the man molded like clay. Dicky was reminded of a mother dressing an infant. Embarrassed, he tiptoed away.

Kathy was irate when he reported to her. She fumed.

"Why, that's horrible. He's no better than a gigolo, accepting all those presents. Poor Ruthie doesn't have the kind of money to do that, and even if she did . . . well, it's just not fair! I'm going to have a talk with that . . . *man* and straighten out a couple of things."

Hesitantly Dicky admitted that he'd never seen the man before and didn't think he was a guest at the hotel. She might have trouble finding him.

"But she said the clothes were for the Sock Hop, right?"

Dicky nodded.

"Then we'll talk to him tonight. At the Sock Hop."

He nodded again. He could see that Kathy had made up her mind, and although he had misgivings—the voice like wind echoed in his ears—he knew from experience that she wasn't the kind of girl you argued with.

Not for an instant had she questioned his botanical origins or suspected him part of some grand prank. All her favorite stories involved handsome men with mysterious pasts, high castle spires ringed with clinging brambles, semisupernatural secrets behind bolted doors. Finding herself in the midst of such a story, she was delighted. In other words, if it was a dream she would rather not be awakened.

She had been, however, slightly embarrassed. After all, a naked man in the middle of the woods. But then he had opened his eyes, and his smile had reassured her. It was all right, anything and everything was all right.

That day after the storm they had passed half an hour smiling while Ruth worked up her nerve. Finally:

"Hi! My name's Ruthie. What's yours?"

This bringing no response, she tried a different tack:

"Bonjour! Je m'appelle Ruth. *Comment ça va?"*

And:

"Buenos días, amigo."

"Buon giorno!"

"Guten Tag?"

She prayed he wasn't Chinese.

He didn't speak until the next day, and then it was in clear, precise English that made Ruth think of rustling leaves.

"I am a gift of love."

That wasn't at all what she had expected. "From who?" she asked. And quickly correcting herself: "From whom?"

"From Earth."

"Oh. Well. What's your name?"

"Call me Can Be and Will."

"Which do you prefer?"

"Will."

"All right, I'll call you Will, and you can call me Ruth, or Ruthie if you like—actually, my name's Ruth Schulman, but Kathy calls me Ruthie—Kathy's my roommate from New York

—I guess you'll meet her sooner or later—she's really beautiful —do you have to stay there? In the middle like that?"

In reply he raised his feet, first left, then right, from the spongy rounded pedestal at the eye of the flower (Ruth could have sworn she heard a tearing sound) and stepped out on one of the long greenish-purple leaves. The leaf lowered under his weight, slowly, until it touched the ground, making a convenient sort of gangplank. He stood beside Ruth, gazing at the now empty bowl of leaves. Under his stare they began to turn autumnal and crumple in on themselves. Soon nothing remained but a dry, nutty brown husk, no bigger than a cocoanut.

Sensing Ruth's disappointment, Will explained, "They have served their purpose. There must be no remorse over things lost. What is given will be taken away; what is taken away returned. There is a balance. Only love is lost. Only love must be renewed."

"I think I understand," Ruth said cautiously. She was surprised; she'd always considered herself stupid; but she *did* understand, as clearly as if the idea had been her own. "It's like everything comes back except the love, and that gets used up, and someone has to come with new love?" She thought for a minute. "It's been a long time since anyone brought new love, hasn't it?"

"A very long time," Will said—sadly, she thought.

She was in awe of him, his perfect knowledge, his beauty. And he didn't seem to mind her. It was a myth propagated by her reading that one day a "pure" man would perceive the doe trapped within her dinosaur body and pledge eternity.

All ugly girls are does within dinosaurs.

It was as if he had read her mind. His cool fingers drew out something dormant in her, something burning and mindless. As she dragged him to the dirt, her mind played a thought like a broken record: If only Kathy could see me now, if only Kathy could see me now, if only. . . .

The Vignettes, a rock-'n'-roll band that had gained overnight stardom in the spring of '56 with their hit single "Four on the Floor and Overhead Cams," and well-deserved oblivion in the fall of that same year, had been resurrected on a platform near the ninth hole. The platform, a fifty-foot wooden raft, floated the grassy waves of the golf course moored by long lines of Japanese lanterns. Occasionally some of the ninety-three dancing survivors would jump overboard and stroll across the greens, an arm around a shoulder, a free hand gesturing with a Schaefer.

The management watched, puzzled but pleased. He remembered the '50s as a time of rigidity, McCarthyism, and the Korean Police Action. But the kids "dug it," he thought philosophically, and invited an idle brunette to dance.

Kathy wore a tight white sweater and a calf-length skirt with a bas-relief poodle on the front; Dicky, a black leather jacket without a shirt. He had greased back his hair with William's Super Pomade.

They had danced three songs when Dicky spotted Ruth and "the man." He said, "That's him," and lindied Kathy sixty degrees so she could have a look without being obvious.

The Vignettes were singing:

> Saw you at the drive-in,
> Dum-be dum-be doo-be
> Looked like you'd been cry-in',
> Dum-be dum-be doo-be

Kathy slowed and stopped like a mechanical toy winding down. Her mouth hung open. Dicky asked her, "What's the matter?" and she shook her head dumbly.

> Couldn't stand to see ya,
> Dum-be dum, so I went
> To the piz-zeria
> Dum-be dum-be doo-be

"Listen, Dicky," Kathy said, "you cut in and dance with Ruth. I'll take her bashful boyfriend and see if I can talk some sense to him."

> I ate a burger and some fri-es,
> Dum-be dum-be, and I
> Thought about your lie-es
> Dum-be dum-be doo-be

Ruth was in ecstasy. Every eye had been on her and beautiful, graceful Will. Now Dicky was cutting in, Kathy's own, who had once called her . . . that awful name. She refused to remember it, for she wasn't like that any more, not since Will had given her the gift of love. She was the belle of the ball. Princes vied for her hand.

"Thank you," she said, while the Vignettes caught their breath. "If you'll excuse me, I'd better get back to Will." She was anxiously scanning the raft.

"Kathy was dancing with him," Dicky said.

Ruth moved through the crowd searching for Will. A boy she recognized, a Ping-Pong-playing insurance salesman from Passaic, was sitting with his girl on the edge of the raft, swinging his legs and talking.

"Sure did," he replied. "They went walking by here about five minutes ago. Looked like they were headed toward the woods."

Ruth felt a creeping panic. She saw a couple far across the golf course, two golden heads shining in the moonlight, and ran after them, rising and falling like flotsam on the slow waves of grass.

"Wait!" she cried breathlessly. "Stop! Oh, Will, I've been looking all over for you . . ."

The boy turned around, and he had a sloping chin and acne; the girl was bony and wore thick glasses.

Ruth mumbled apologies.

Couples everywhere; only Ruth was alone. She shut herself in her room; she threw herself on the bed; she pleaded with the pillow.

"He was *mine*. . . . *I* found him and *I* went out there every day and talked to him. . . . *I* bought him those clothes . . . and she's already got a boyfriend, she has lots of them and I only had Will . . . it's not right . . . it's not fair. . . ."

At breakfast, Ruth swore she would never again speak to him. Kathy sat alone two tables away, digging at a grapefruit. They didn't look at each other. *Even if he came crawling back on his beautiful knees.* She stopped a waiter and ordered every other item on the morning menu. She always ate a lot in situations like this. *Just let him try.*

At lunch Ruth thought she just might forgive him if he asked her the right way. Kathy and Dicky were at the other end of the dining room laughing about something. *After all, he was very special. A gift of love.* Feeling better, she skipped dessert.

Later she took a walk in the woods, not to see Will, but if she happened to run into him . . . well.

He was waiting on a rock in the clearing where the plant had been.

"Ha ha ha, you'll never believe this," Ruth said gaily, sitting down next to him. "When I couldn't find you last night, I thought you'd gone off with Kathy."

"I had," Will replied.

"No, but I thought the two of you did something together. Isn't that silly?"

"We came back here. We made love."

Abruptly Ruth got up and turned away. She was crying, waiting for him to come over and comfort her, to tell her it didn't mean anything, a one-night stand, lust, not love, etc. But Will wasn't trained in the theater of contemporary interpersonal relationships. He didn't know his part, so he sat where he was and hummed:

> Saw you at the drive-in,
> Dum-be, dum-be doo-be

Sadness fermented into anger. Ruth whirled around and accused him: "Well, don't you have anything to say for yourself? Don't you think you owe me an apology or at the very least an explanation? Well?"

She waited, arms akimbo on her broad hips. Broad as a battleship.

"I don't understand," Will said. His eyes were obdurate but warm, as if they'd been chiseled from marble. Examining them, she knew that he was being completely honest. He really didn't understand. This wasn't in her favorite stories; it hadn't happened in her limited experience with boys; in fact, it was probably unique to the history of Western man—an encounter with a *tabula rasa* mind that understood neither guilt nor moral prohibitions. So Ruth dealt with it as best she could; she abandoned herself to impulse. And her impulse was to grab Will by the arm and drag him to her room.

"I am supposed to stay here," Will said. "I am supposed to meet Kathy."

"No! No, that's no good. Don't you see?"

"Why is it no good?"

She was pulling him across the golf course. They passed the insurance salesman from Passaic, who was excavating a sand trap. A second party shunted by them in a motorized red golf cart. The sun was very hot.

"It's no good because—" the first thing that popped into her head— "because she's trying to kill you. Yes. She and Dicky. It's a plot. They're jealous of us."

"Jealous?"

"Just take my word for it."

Ruth was afraid of meeting Kathy in the lobby. Her heart beating very quickly, she ran Will past the checkout desk to the stairwell. She locked the door to her room behind her, the bathroom door; then she closed the Venetian blinds. Will stood in the middle of the room watching.

"We're going to stay right here," Ruth said, "and we'll both be very happy." She locked the door to the bathroom. "Can you play checkers?"

"What is checkers?" Will said.

"I'll teach you. There's a checker set in the rec room. I'll go get it. And I'll get some magazines, and we'll have our meals sent up."

Ruth felt much better.

Will lay on the bed. He was weak. His skin had become an unpleasant pasty texture, his eyes dull and opaque, as if chiseled from granite.

Ruth sat next to him, the checkerboard on her lap. She was worried, but she put on a gay mask and reminded him, "It's your move."

With an effort he propped himself on one arm and surveyed the board.

"That wasn't a very good move," Ruth said. "You see, now I can jump you here, and here, and here and get kinged. You're not feeling so good, are you?"

"No."

Ruth brushed aside his golden curls and felt his forehead. It was cold and damp.

"You'll feel better tomorrow," she said.

But he didn't. Ruth noticed that his fingertips and toes were darkening and the skin had begun to wrinkle.

The next day Will could no longer pick up the plastic checkers. When he tried, his shriveled fingers bent backward with a crackling sound. Ruth made him lie down and read him a condensed novel from *Cosmopolitan.*

Ruth always cracked her door and took a peek before using the bathroom. If Kathy's door was opened, Ruth would shut it quickly, silently, with one gesture. She dreaded confronting Kathy. Kathy, on the other hand, seemed to have forgotten Will, the night in the woods, the entire incident. On several occasions she called through the door to ask if Ruth was all right. "After saving up all year . . ." Kathy would say, and "There's a lecture on organic cooking. Are you sure you wouldn't like to come?"

Will's hair began to fall out. He seemed to be growing smaller, his arms and legs retracting. His skin was loose, brown, crazed with intricate wrinkles. Three fingers dropped off. Ruth tried to stick them back with Johnson & Johnson First Aid Tape.

Ruth gave him aspirins and cold compresses. Will accepted without questioning.

"Isn't there anything I can do to help you?" she moaned. "Won't anything make you better?"

"Sunlight and air, earth and water." His voice was like the wind whistling through a rocky canyon.

"But if you go outside, they'll kill you. They're jealous. Don't you understand?"

"I have died before. I will be again. Life is conserved."

Ruth rented a sun lamp from a store in town. She sprinkled water on Will's body. She brought up a tub of dirt, and Kathy called through the door, "For heaven's sake, Ruthie, we're only going to be here two more days. Wouldn't you like to come down to the pool? They're giving scuba-diving lessons all afternoon and the equipment's free!"

Will was tiny, a wizened old man in an oversized sack of skin. His dark chestnut color reminded Ruth of ancient people she had seen embalmed on Miami beaches. His right hand fell off, and Ruth, at a loss, disposed of it the way she had dead goldfish when she was little. Down the toilet. The hand would meet the goldfish in the sewers of Pennsylvania.

He looked dead; he hadn't twitched or spoken or blinked in twelve hours. With mild revulsion, Ruth pressed her hand to the charred knot of skin that had once been his chest and felt for rhythms of life. She switched off the sun lamp with the same finality a doctor would an iron lung.

The moonlight showed her way across the slow waves of the golf course. She carried what was left of Will in a sheet in her arms. It was very light, surprisingly light. She knew the way through the woods. Kneeling, she burrowed with her hands. Her palms bled into the dirt. The hole was four feet deep. She left no marker.

Dicky offered to drive them back to New York. They took the top down on Kathy's tomato-soup Volkswagen convertible and cruised along country roads, past barns with hex signs and Amish in their surreys, dressed in black, perpetually mourning. Ruth sat in the back with the luggage.

"Whatever happened," Kathy began, but changed her mind. It was such a beautiful day. "I'm glad I have you for a friend," she said instead.

Dicky, being diplomatic, agreed.

Ruth went back to teaching kindergarten and had a good year. One day in the fall the new supervisor stopped by to observe her and stayed after class to invite her for dinner. He was a hulking man named Fred, with a passion for loud ties and a peculiar tenderness when he spoke about the children: "You think Franny Weiss is developing antisocial patterns?" Something about Ruth, a sad quality of things lost, attracted him. They dated often and the subject of marriage was discussed on several occasions.

In June he suggested a weekend in the country. Ruth told him about a place she knew near the Pocono Mountains, in Pennsylvania.

Three miles from Hideaway in the Poconos they took a wrong turn (it seemed clear as yesterday to Ruth, but try as she might she couldn't recall if it was the left fork or straight ahead) and came to a little roominghouse with a weather cock and green shutters. Ruth was enchanted. The proprietress baked mince pies and left them on the sill to cool. Fred phoned Hideaway in the Poconos and canceled their reservations.

The second day of their stay they drove over to Hideaway in the Poconos. Proud Ruth introduced Fred to the management, who didn't remember her but pretended he did. They went for a walk in the woods. Lichen carpeted their feet and a recent rain had raised patches of doughy mushrooms.

Ruth was kneeling, holding the earth, and between her hands a peculiar pine cone, greenish purple in color, stood nearly a foot high.

Gazing at it, Ruth imagined a girl, miserable and alone as she herself had once been, discovering the earthblossom and learning the same tragic lesson: that love cannot survive imprisoned, that love must be free to thrive. And the risk of abandonment must be lived with, even though it is as frightening as death.

"She'll have to kill it," whispered a wiser Ruth.

Fred did not understand, but sensing this was a special, private moment, he did not interrupt. He waited till later, while they were crossing the golf course, for the question he had been so long working up his courage to ask. She happily agreed. Yet during the following fifty-two years they would spend together, finding comfort in each other while a world fell apart at the seams, he was never to learn the true significance of that moment.

"Sing that song again, Orpheus," Hercules repeated. "By the way, Linus the music-master, whom in self-defense, long ago, I brained with his own lyre—a tiresome pedant—was he not your brother?"

"Forget those dark deeds, Hercules," said Orpheus sorrowfully, and presently struck up again.

—Robert Graves, *Hercules, My Shipmate*

YELLOWHEAD

BY JACK DANN AND GEORGE ZEBROWSKI

The subway train was a flash of salad colors as Retro Five, recently acquired by The Henchmen's Sixth Division, pulled into the Bedford Park Station. That was where they let Yellowhead off for the last time, only twenty-three years after the trains had been painted and taken over by the Pain 5 People, who run them to this day better than the uptop jobbers. Black Satin and Stitch Tonto hijacked the first train one long-ago summer, moved their Pilots into the last car, called it Smoke Three and ran it up and down the line. Soon no one cared.

Yellowhead started with Retro Five, then left for Jerome Avenue to run his own operation. All the best painters followed him. No one saw him upside after he shaved his head and painted it yellow. He had a red, freckled face, a long, overly thin nose, thick sensuous lips and a weak chin that showed a slight cleft. He was more than six feet tall and lanky, always bending over, slouching as if he needed to bend toward the security of a floor.

With his painted head and tinted body, he was an awesome sight to the busy people—the fingermen and serfage workers and layers and prompters and factory-sitters. Although their jobs were high and low, they all dressed the same: white-roughed faces, eyes lined, noses shadowed, hair bristled and bronzed—lacking all natural color—starched white shirts and snake black ties, tricolor jackets and pantaloons.

But Yellowhead couldn't stand the sameness of ties and jobs, sametalk and samesex, so he smoked some of Mama's Pain 5 and cut his neatly cropped hair. To substitute for his lack of color, he dipped into a paint store and covered himself with yellow. He almost died that first time, for he didn't realize that the body, like the lungs, had to breathe. He was barked and beaten

35

twice that day, and gang-raped once, before he fled to the subways—his secret dream, that "slum hole for degenerates and filth," as Mama used to say.

Yellowhead had a darling, but he didn't know it until too late. Her name was Yoy Cross and she was as fair as a white line.

Yoy Cross, straight as they came and full of cliches, was a seamworker in North Brunswick Section Factory on 53rd Street. She had glint-gilded hair, trussed and tied as was the summer fashion, a fair face like Yellowhead's, but with thin lips and dimple creases. She was short and slight, small-boned and delicate. She had been trained to drive country trucks and largecars, but she had fallen from grace by refusing to manage company affairs and had left in virgin haste. Her Borndaddy and sister had thrown her out of the house as an example to the neighbors. She would have the stigma of a "Cherry" even after she had been bobbed by as many men and loving women as she could hold. She was a tragic throwback.

Six days a week she rode the Retro Five and watched the painters working their designs and graffiti onto the metal walls —inside and outside. That was her break in the day's monotony, her flash of danger. The dark tunnels promised to swallow her, promised juicy, delicious night-terrors. And the bare, bright ceiling bulbs provided security.

"Okay, okay, okay, okay," shouted a twelve-year-old dressed in khakis and dirty shirt. He brandished a crowbar, but not menacingly. He was polite and pushed his way through the crowd until he could get near enough to a handhold. He hooked his crowbar onto the handhold and swung back and forth with one arm, kicking an uptown woman in the shoulder. She only sighed and moved away. It was the weekend; everyone wanted to get home and rest—the insecurity of the subway could be least tolerated on Saturday. Even Yoy looked down at the painted floor and wished for home and toilet.

"Okay, okay, okay," shouted another boy, older than the other, but dressed the same. He passed Yoy, purposely stepping on her foot and smiling and waving his crowbar. "Excuse me, pardon me, sorry, sorry . . ."

Yoy looked around for a Pilot but couldn't find one. This car was dislocated; there was not even a painter to add contrast and safety, just upsiders like herself, and no one to protect them from themselves.

The train pushed through the tunnels, curving, climbing, turning, then screeched—metal against metal—and slowed down before a red light. It bolted, ran for a few seconds and jerked to another stop. Through the smeared windows Yoy could see the roundtop intersection: bare bulbs shining wanly in a garage pit, cement struts crisscrossed with metal tiebars, other tunnels—illusions of immensity, leaders of track and another waiting train pulled up. It was close enough to touch, a metal dragon of green and yellow and red, a sandblast paint job, car after car painted and pruned to look like a Wu-dragon, a metal centipede. That had been painted before Yellowhead had left Retro Five—a good time when the best painters could still be boasted by Stitch Tonto.

Yoy hoped this wouldn't be a long stop. The air would become thick and some old man would start coughing and wheezing and start everyone else crying and sneezing and screaming. Someone died in her car at least once every week. She thought perhaps she was a jinx, a laylow, but then so was everyone else.

"Hey, Cherry, Cherry," screamed a high-pitched male voice. Yoy turned around, saw it was an old neighbor's son. He was still fat and pimply, and his face was dirty except for paint spots and drool lines. She tried to ignore him. He had joined a gang of boys with crowbars, but he was young and green so was only permitted to carry a broken umbrella stick. She was sure that would make him mean.

"Hey, lolly, lolly, Yoy," sang another boy. They all pushed toward her, bars in hand, hair plastered back unstylishly, mouths puckered in polite smiles.

The youngest boy tried his luck on a young girl—slashed her face with an umbrella end, rubbed her belly and humped her. The crowd looked through the windows, grumbled and kept at smalltalk. After all, the boys were still being polite.

Next an old man. His wife was too stiff to scream. Dress the same, rape the same—that was the time-honored jingo.

An older boy—sword scar across his face down to his neck, blue eyes that twinkled, greased hair in ringlets and unpainted mouth with no teeth—pushed into Yoy, ripped the front of her dress open and watched to see if the boy beside her intended to help her. He looked away, and the older boy ground glass knuckles into Yoy's face. With fairly good style, he bloodied both her breasts and then proceeded to rape her slowly.

Yoy screamed, pretended she wasn't there, stared out the window as the dragon train pulled away silently, its cars jerking under its painted carapace.

But it was too soon for Yoy to black out. Virginity can be taken only once, and she, through her tears and screams, was enjoying her betrothal to society. Offspring from such a union would be considered holy, but she knew she wouldn't tell her family. Let them cross and snuffle in their rotten rooms.

With a jerk, the train started moving. She could feel him shaking like a weak child and was amused that such a fragile husk was forcing itself into her.

More screams—her own.

And unknown to her, a few boys, painted and plumed, jumped across from the rear car to the tunnel catwalk, heading for the club cave near the old pipe junction.

He got off her as the train started to roar into the tunnel. The car was empty, and she could tell that he was disappointed. His audience had fled into the forward parts of the train.

That was when Yellowhead came into the car, walking forward on his rounds, checking the car links and open-close door whooshers. She saw him come up behind the thief and bring his fist down on his head, crumpling him with one blow.

She opened her eyes and tried to sit up. She tried to grab Yellowhead's hand, but he only smiled.

"You'll be happy without him," he said to her.

And she felt that he wanted her. He had fought for her, however slightly. He continued into the next car as she fixed herself up. She watched him go, but she knew that when next they met, it would be different. He was being kind now, leaving her to her rites, content to wait for when they would meet on more individual terms.

But he never spoke to her again.

She rode his train week after week, hoping to catch a glimpse of him. She listened to conversations about him on the other lines. And she followed him when rumor told her that he was riding elsewhere in the city with friends in their living cars at the ends of their trains. Once through a car window she saw him change his clothes. For a moment she caught a glimpse of his tattooed body topped by his yellow skull. He was thin and wiry and could not see her in the dark tunnel where she stood. She had come up to the window too late for him to see her.

As time went on her love became more anxious. He did not notice her even when she smiled at him. She became desperate when he disappeared for a whole month during the short war with the out-city trains. He came back with a bandage over his right eye and his arm in a sling, and she cried for his pain.

Now his indifference was slowly turning into betrayal in her mind. The saddest songs come from this part of her life. The train howls in the tunnel and the wheels whine more sweetly than an electric violin. The air in the tunnels vibrates with the tears of heroes.

And a train comes rolling forward toward the woman who must die. She has chained herself to the track. The train cuts her in half like a razor and stops.

Yellowhead is called out to see the body. He sees the face and her tattered dress, her hands flung outward over the third rail, which flickers with blue life under her divided form.

The train pulls into the Bedford Station, and Yellowhead gets off to stand on the platform. The downtown train pulls in and he sees her words written in red across two cars.

I LOVE YOU YELLOWHEAD
MY NAME IS YOY

Then he remembers the time in the train when she had looked up at him, reaching out for his hand as he walked away. He moves to the end of the platform and looks back into the mouth of death, where the blue flashes still light the darkness —on and off, on and off, with the smell of ozone and burnt flesh pushing out at him.

At that moment he leaped down onto the tracks and began walking slowly into the darkness. Those who saw him for the last time remember, finally, only his yellow skull bright in the blackness.

No one ever found a body. No one ever found Yoy. No one knows how he picked her up from the electrified rail without falling down dead beside it. Some say he went down into the maze of tunnels, into the caves beneath the river, to rest with her; and their bones still lie there in dry embrace.

Some say they see Yellowhead grinning at them in the high-speed tunnels of the booster trains. They say his ghost lives in the magnetic field that propels the new trains, that it is summoned away from Yoy's arms when the train passes over their place deep in the undercity.

The songs say that nothing in life moved Yellowhead so much as finding out that she had loved him. Others say that he would not have loved her at all if he had not learned too late that she was lost to him. For him to notice, the missing part of his life had to die.

Now there are trains on the moon, under it and above, boosters and surface monorail. And there is a new song which says that Yellowhead's ghost is in all the metal made on earth; and wherever trains rush, Yellowhead will slip from Yoy's bony clasp to go and look at them. Recently his giant ghost was seen sitting on the rim of a crater, looking up at the stars, dreaming of tunnels across the heavens. A legend is the loveliest part of the truth.

Other songs say different things.

There are men in the village of Erith
Whom nobody seeth or heareth,
    And there looms, on the marge
    Of the river, a barge
That nobody roweth or steereth.

—Mother Goose

PUDDLE ON THE FLOOR

BY R. A. LAFFERTY

1

Petronilla heard two different giggles in the den. These had to come from two different boys, for they were going on at the same time. Oh, she'd catch them now! She hurried to pounce on the situation.

And the phone rang just as she opened the den door. And the doorbell rang. They always rang just when she was about to— A fast look through the door showed another boy in the den with Gregory, that dirty slinky little boy she'd almost seen so many times before. But the phone jangled with rising anger, and the doorbell absolutely boomed.

"Yes, yes," she told the phone. "Anemia, is it? The doctor is sure? I never heard of a cat getting anemia before. Patsy, I've got somebody at the front door, and I'm about to catch Greg in something rotten at the same time. I'll call you back."

"Yes, yes," she told the opened front door then. "Yes, Hermione. Anemia, is it? That's what Patsy Pettegolezzo's cat's got too. Oh, Hermione, I'm just about to have a row with Greg. Go on through to the kitchen. The coffee's on and the cinnamon rolls are in the warming oven."

Now, now, had Petronilla let the situation escape her? No, she had not. She still heard the second voice and the second giggle in the den, and the only way out of the den was that one door. The boys had it closed again, of course, but she could hear two of them inside. And then—

"Quick, quick, go, go, she's come back already," little Greg screamed inside as Petronilla's hand was on the knob. She threw the door wide open, and her son Greg was alone inside, absolutely alone. She knew every place in that den that was big

43

enough to hide a little boy, and she knew that the door she held in her hand was the only way out. There had been another little boy in the room. He hadn't come out. And he wasn't in there now.

"Who was with you just now in the den, Greg?" she asked with her smooth-shoed voice.

"There wasn't anybody with me. I talk to myself and I practice two voices."

"But I *saw* the other boy, Greg. And then the phone and the door both rang. And I heard him in here just before I opened the door this time. Talk in two voices, do you? Let me hear you do it now!"

"I can't do it now, mama. Only sometimes."

"Why do you lie to me, Greg?"

"Believe me, mama, sometimes you get in holes and lying's the only way out."

"And does it get you out of the holes, Greg?"

"It helps, mama."

"Oh, Greg! Another puddle on the floor! Why do you *do* it? You're a big boy six years old."

"It isn't what you think it is, mama."

"Greg, I am going to have to have answers to a few questions right now."

"What are they?"

"Who *is* the little boy who was with you, the little boy who appears and disappears?"

"What's the other questions?"

"Why and how do you make puddles on the floor? Your pants are never wet. This is either very deliberate of you, or it is something else entirely."

"It's something else entirely, mama. What's the other questions?"

"What got all the cats in the neighborhood? And the dogs and the birds? And the hamsters and the rabbits and the turtles? What is it that's getting all the pets, and what is it doing with them?"

"Nothing's been getting them right lately, mama."

"That's because they were all got. And the new ones that the people have been buying now, no, they haven't been disappearing, but they've been getting sick. What could give anemia to

Patsy Pettegolezzo's cat and to Hermione Greygoose's too?"

"Strega O'Conner is giving the cats anemia now, I guess. She's spreading it around and not taking all of it from any of them, so it won't kill them."

"Strega O'Conner gives me the willies, but how could she give anemia to cats?"

"Is that one of the questions, mama?"

"No, not right now it isn't. But it probably will be."

"What's the rest of the questions then? I'm in kind of a hurry."

"Don't tell me that you're in a hurry, little boy. But another question is how is it possible for one six-year-old boy to eat so much bran for breakfast? There's been thirteen boxes already this week, and this is only Wednesday. What do you *do* with all of it?"

"What's the other questions, mama?"

"That's enough of them for right now. Oh, I wish your father were still alive. He'd get to the bottom of this."

"I bet he wouldn't. He was never very good at getting anything out of me."

"All right, let's have some answers, young man."

Both the phone and the door began to ring, loudly and with great determination. Petronilla Ashling started to answer them. And then she stopped suddenly and turned back to her son.

"Greg, make the phone and the door both stop ringing, right now!"

"How could I make them stop ringing? I never heard of such a thing."

"You made them start ringing. You *did!* And you made them ring the other time too."

"Yes, I did. But I can't make them stop."

"Why not?"

"Because there really is somebody on the phone. And there really is somebody at the door. There was somebody on them the other time too, wasn't there?"

"Yes. But how do you make them ring whenever you want to and have real people there when I answer them?"

"I don't know how I do it, mama. But I can tell you that they won't stop ringing till you answer them now. It makes me nervous when you let them ring like that."

"There's a lot of things making me nervous around here lately," Petronilla told her son. She answered the phone. She told the real person who was on it to wait a minute. She answered the door. And between these two calls she was involved for fifteen minutes. She heard Greg go out doors. She heard that little girl Strega O'Conner across the street singing a jump-rope rhyme:

"This is the puddle, shallow and gray.
A gentleman drowned in it today."

Petronilla Ashling wrung her hands and puzzled her head. That little girl Strega drove her up walls with her chants, but how could the chants give cats anemia? And how could they do things much more suspicious? Petronilla had her front-door caller talking to her telephone caller now (they were friends), and she heard that they were talking about their cats and dogs having anemia.

Petronilla thought about sick cats now, and she recalled that the problem of the previous week had been the catnapper stealing and killing all the cats and other pets of the neighborhood. She thought about the puddles of water on the floor and about the empty bran boxes in the kitchen. How was it possible for Greg to eat as many as five one-pound boxes of wheat bran for breakfast and she not be able to see him eat any of them? How was it possible for him to eat all that and still be so skinny?

"If his father was still alive I'd push the problems off on him," Petronilla said. "How can he make the phone and the door both ring whenever he wants to distract me from questioning him? And how can he make there to be real people there when I answer? Oh, which end of this horrible mess will I start with? Where will I catch hold of it? I will catch hold of that other little boy by the ears or the neck—that's where I'll catch hold of it. I will use the dirtiest trick in the world."

Entrapment is the dirtiest trick in the world. Petronilla would set a trap, and she would watch and wait. She had been afraid to ask Greg about the peanut butter jars full of blood (it looked like blood). She had asked him more intermediate questions, but this one would have to be asked in some form. It would be the bait for the trap. Whenever Greg was out of jars of blood, then he was also out of the other little boy. And whenever he had a jar or two of the chocolate-cherry-colored stew, then that dirty and slinky little boy would appear again very soon. But where did that blood come from?

Oh, that little Strega O'Conner was singing another jump-rope rhyme across the street. ("If I were her mother I'd knock her heads together," Petronilla said.) And the rhyme, as all of Strega's, was very loud:

> "Cat in the catchy-bag, thud, thud, thud!
> Come get the freshy stuff, blood, blood, blood."

So, then, was little Strega O'Conner trafficking in blood? Was that the answer to it?

In less than half an hour Strega O'Conner came over to the Ashlings bringing some cookies that her mother had made. She brought them and nothing else. Petronilla never took her eyes off of that child. Strega came over four more times that day, and she didn't bring any blood into the house. Was all this an illusion?

"Oh, if my husband were still alive, what would he do about these problems?" Petronilla moaned. "He'd guffaw his silly head off at them, that's what he'd do."

Petronilla even dreamed about it that night. She dreamed that Strega O'Conner slipped into the house during the night with three peanut butter jars full of blood. And Petronilla woke in the early morning to a thudding sound. It was the paper boy throwing the morning paper on the porch. Then Petronilla was out of bed like a taking-off bird and to the window. She knew that somebody had *made* the paper boy thud the paper just at that moment to disguise another sound, the sound of a door closing. And there was Strega, who had just slipped out of the Ashling house in the early morning and was going across to her own house. Petronilla went to her son's bedside, and there on his night stand were three peanut butter jars full of what might very well be blood.

"All right, then," she said. "The little boy will come again this morning, though I'm afraid to make the connection between the blood and his coming. I will make a big stir around. I will say that I'm going to be doing the washing in the basement. And

I will set the washing noises to going there. But I will not be in the basement. I will be watching, watching, watching by my trap. But first, before I get Greg up and get him his breakfast, before I set the washer to going, I will do two other things."

Petronilla Ashling disconnected her phone from the phone jack. And she disconnected her door bell at the push button at the front door.

She called Greg to get up, and he mumbled something behind the closed door of his room. She opened that door suddenly. The jars of blood were no longer on the little night stand. He had hidden them somewhere. Greg was pretending to be still half asleep, but he was only pretending.

Petronilla tried to catch her son Greg at it at breakfast. He was always too fast for her. She would look away for a moment, and a box of bran would be clear empty. She would look away for another moment, and another box of bran would be done away with.

"How can you eat so much bran, Greg?" she asked. But with the fifth box of it she saw what happened. Greg had a catchy-bag of his own, and that's where he put the bran. He wasn't eating any of it. Petronilla pretended not to have seen this, and she went down to the basement as soon as breakfast was over. And then she crept up again and listened at the door of the den, where Greg had shut himself up.

She heard his giggle. She heard another little boy's giggle. She put her hand on the knob of the door and—

"Petronilla, your phone isn't working!" Patsy Pettegolezzo called from the window.

"Petronilla, your doorbell isn't working!" Hermione Greygoose called from the front door.

"Oh, perish you, kind neighbors!" Petronilla exploded, and she refused to be diverted. She swung the den door open. She grabbed that strange little boy by an ear and by the back of his neck and she dragged him out of there.

"Mama, the phone's ringing and the doorbell's ringing!" Gregory cried. But they weren't, or they weren't ringing very much. Even Greg could not make disconnected bells ring clearly or with authority.

Petronilla dragged that dirty, slinky little boy out of the house, jerking him by arm and shoulder now and whacking him on the seat of the pants at every step. And yet she couldn't say what he was guilty of.

"That's mean, mama, he hasn't done anything," Greg was calling and following along behind. And that slinky little boy dragged his feet and tried to hold onto things to keep from being dragged along.

Then (horror!) Petronilla pulled an arm clear off the little boy. In a moment she was flushed with confusion and fear. And Strega O'Conner across the street was jumping rope and singing a jump-rope rhyme:

"This is the boy who got his wish.
We'll eat him alive in a porridge dish."

The little boy was crying and beginning to cave in.

"You'd better go now, Eugene," Gregory said. "I'll get you back here again in a couple of days."

"All right," the strange little boy said. He collapsed still more. Petronilla tried to straighten him up. The other arm and part of the shoulder came off him, and both Patsy and Hermione were watching it all. The head fell off the little boy and rolled on the sidewalk there. And several more people were watching now.

"Oh, I've never had it like this before," Petronilla moaned. "I could just perish from confusion!"

But it was the strange little boy who perished. He disintegrated. He melted clear down. And there was nothing left of him but a puddle of water on the sidewalk. And all of those busy-bee people were closing in to see what it was all about.

"Brazen it out, mama," Gregory whispered. "That's what I always do when I'm caught with it."

"What little boy?" Petronilla asked innocently when people began to question her.

"What little boy?" Gregory Ashling asked them all.

"What little boy?" Strega O'Conner asked, coming from across the street and still jumping rope. Strega was as brazen as a six-year-old girl could be. And, after some draggy and embarrassing moments, the busy people went away jabbering.

But when they were alone together Greg complained to his mother about her conduct.

"He melts when you scare him or when you're rough with him," Greg said. "I don't know whether you know it, but that's the third time this week that you've made him melt. And then you blame me for using so much bran!"

"Ah, I don't seem able to go on with these weird things any longer," Petronilla snuffled. "What we will have to do, Gregory, is get a new father for you. Then he can be responsible for these things."

"I don't want a new father," Gregory protested. "I don't like any of the men that you like."

"You will like this one, Gregory," Petronilla said, "or it will be your own fault. You can have him just the way you want him."

2

"Yes, that is what I mean, Gregory," Petronilla said to her son. "You can select every quality you want in your father. You can make him just the way that you want him to be, or at least I think that you can. I trust your judgment and your taste. I will abide by your decision. I know the things that you have been making, and I know that you can make a grown man."

"It sure will take a lot of bran, mama. It takes a lot for even a little boy."

"The sky is the limit as far as bran is concerned," Petronilla said. "However much bran it takes, we will get it."

"And it sure will take a lot of blood. I'm scared of it. I never made anybody except little boys before."

"As to the blood, make whatever arrangements are necessary with Strega O'Conner, dear. If she needs more peanut butter jars to put it in, then we will get more for her. If she needs more blood than she can get from the cats and dogs around here, then we will get her a hog or a cow or something with a lot of blood in it. Now you be thinking very hard about just what you want in a father. Make him as nearly perfect as you can."

"All right, mama."

"Do you know what his name will be?"

"Oh sure. It will be Greatheart Noble."

"Fine. I like that name," Petronilla Ashling said. "I'll go get the marriage license now. And I'll go get something else." She went out to go about her errands, and she waved across the street in a new friendly fashion to Strega O'Conner, who was jumping rope and singing a rhyme:

"This is the wife who lost her man,
And made her another from blood and bran."

The next morning, Petronilla Ashling was thrilled and chilled at the sight of her new man Greatheart Noble. Greatheart was very tall, and he wore some kind of shako on his head. He had hussar mustaches, and he was chested like a pouter pigeon. He wore a scarlet and purple cape and a scarlet and gold tunic, and he was belted and booted in black leather. He carried a ring-master's whip in his hand. He was quite handsome in some old stylized and costumed fashion. He gave crisp green money to Gregory.

"Go buy toy soldiers," he said.

He gave crisp green money to Petronilla.

"Go buy toy dishes and toy tea service," he said.

"No, no, I'm not a little girl," she explained. "I'm a big girl, but I'll keep the money. Come along now. We're going to City Hall to be married."

"Will it hurt?" Greatheart asked. He gave more crisp money to Gregory.

"Go buy nuts. Go buy candy. Go buy ice skates. Go buy a pony," he said.

"We love your money, Greatheart," Petronilla said, "but come, come, come! It's time for us to get married."

"Don't scare him, mama, or he'll melt," Gregory cautioned. "Don't be rough with him. Don't frustrate him at all. Take all the money he wants to give you or he'll feel frustrated."

"I will be very careful of him," Petronilla said. "With thirty-one boxes of bran and a whole hog invested in him, I will be most careful. And I'll not frustrate him by refusing his money. Come, dear Greatheart, it's married we will be."

Petronilla Ashling and Greatheart Noble went out into the street, past a dead hog that was there, a completely empty-looking dead hog (it had all the blood drained out of it), and down the street to City Hall.

"It comes to me that I don't know where I am or what I'm doing here," Greatheart said in his vaguely foreign voice. He gave Petronilla considerable money.

"Buy a coach and eight," he said. "Buy a footman and a postboy and a driver and four outriders."

"Thank you, dear Greatheart. I'll buy better things than those."

"I find myself among strange people in a strange land," Greatheart said. "I am ensorcelled by sorcerers."

"Yeah, I know," Petronilla said. "Let's hurry before it wears off." They came to City Hall. They were married without particular incident, though there was some tittering about Greatheart flicking his ringmaster's whip during the ceremony.

And then they made another stop, to finalize the insurance policies that Petronilla was taking out on her new husband. Greatheart passed his physical examination and was declared to be a perfect specimen ("Of what I'm not sure," the examining doctor said) and was stated to be the best risk ever seen. (Petronilla had been afraid that they'd discover that he had pig's blood.)

"Is it like a lottery tournament?" Greatheart asked at the insurance office. He gave Petronilla huge bunches of very large money. "Bet more on me, then," he said. "In Transylvania it is the grandest men who have the most bet on them."

And Petronilla gladly increased the premium payment and then increased it again.

And this was the beginning of the happiest three days ever in the life of Petronilla Ashling Noble. Greatheart wouldn't stand too close an examination, of course. In no detail was he really accurate, in some things he was ridiculous (like something a six-year-old boy would have thought of), and in other areas he was completely blank.

"I'll just quit wearing my glasses, and then it'll be all right," Petronilla said. "I never cared too much for fine detail anyhow."

So Petronilla and Greatheart began to give parties and bashes to celebrate their nuptials and their new roles in local society. They gave a "We Got Married" party, a "Welcome Greatheart" party, a "Honeymoon Buffet" party, and others. It was the same circle of friends who came to all of them: Clovis and Patsy

Pettegolezzo, Grantland and Hermione Greygoose, Craig and Thecla Petersen, Driscol and Hyacinth Oldking, Adolph and Clementine O'Conner. And, of course, their little girl Strega O'Conner could not be kept out.

And there's no doubt that Greatheart Noble made a strong impression at these parties, and Petronilla herself was the perfect picture of Pride Fulfilled. Greatheart was crude in some of his efforts ("You like it?" he asked Driscol Oldking, who gaped at the new Noble sports car. "Here, go get one for yourself." And there was the cramming out of crisp, green hundred-dollar and thousand-dollar bills), but he was crude in the way of one who has a royal right to such crudity.

And there's no doubt that Greatheart was unbelievably boyish and was the most flamboyant showboat ever seen. It would take only one "Show them your muscles, papa" from Gregory for tall and chesty Greatheart to throw off his scarlet and golden tunic and his scarlet and purple cape and strike the pose and send the rippling mountains of his muscles through their paces. But was there something wrong about those muscles?

"I will admit I've never seen anything like them," Driscol Oldking said, "but they're not valid. They're like burlesques of muscles, like caricatures. They're like balloons instead of sinews. They're like pictures of muscles as a little boy might draw them."

"I know," said Clovis Pettegolezzo, "but what does it matter?"

Greatheart had Tokay wines of obscure vintage, and sour milk dishes, and other specialties of Hungary and Rumania and Greece and Turkey flown in. He served a true Transylvanian board, with racked ribs of wolf as a main dish all three evenings. And Petronilla had all fill-in things catered by Mike McGoogan's Elite Catering Service. They had in a three-person combo to play for them on fiddle and piano and drums. And they made sparkling presentations of all they did. For three days and nights they were sparkling.

But Greatheart wasn't as costumed a figure as he seemed, for sometimes he did speak searchingly and out of character.

"I'm confused, confused," he said to Driscol Oldking once. "I'm like a man in a dream, but I've always believed that a man was responsible for everything, even his dreams. I'm a person under sorcery; and all of you here are, to me, parts of the sorcerers' world. I believe that my real body is still sleeping in my castle in Transylvania" (They cannot wake me up, they cannot wake me! What if they bury me as dead when they cannot wake me?) "and that only a vagrant portion of my sleeping self is present here in a way that I can't understand. Here is money, Driscol. Go to an alchemist or apothecary and see if you can buy a remedy for my condition."

Driscol Oldking took the money from Greatheart, but he did not find a remedy for his condition anywhere.

But after three days of celebrating Petronilla turned a little bit disappointed.

"I wonder if you could make an adjustment in your father, Gregory?" she asked.

"I don't know what, mama. He's perfect, isn't he?"

"Oh, I suppose so. But, ah, in one way he just doesn't work."

"I put in everything I could think of he ought to have. What does it matter if he doesn't work, mama? He gives us lots more money than fathers who do work."

"I don't mean 'to work for a living.' I mean like 'to work, to function.' "

"I don't understand what you mean, mama."

Strega O'Conner across the street was jumping a rhyme:

> "This is the man unblessed by kirk,
> But something about the man don't work."

"Strega understands what I mean," Petronilla said.

"No wonder. She's a week older than I am. But if you're through with Greatheart, mama, then we'll get rid of him and I'll make someone else."

"Are you going to make that dirty little boy again? Can't you make someone else and still keep Greatheart? We will get more bran."

"No, I won't make Eugene again. He was getting in trouble at home going into those trances. But I want to make someone else. No, I can just make one of them at a time. I can't make anyone else till Greatheart is unmade."

"But I'd like to keep him," Petronilla said, "even if he doesn't work in every respect. I'm getting attached to him."

"Mama, don't do that. You know he isn't real. He's like one of the figures on Huppett's Puppets. And anyway aren't you getting a little bit anxious to—"

"To cash him in? Yes, I guess I am. What would happen if we had him run over with a car?"

"He'd melt."

"What would happen if we poisoned him?"

"Nothing. He wouldn't poison."

"What would happen if we had an unknown gunman shoot him?"

"He'd melt. I think that everybody melts a little bit if you scare them bad enough."

"Oh yes, there's an old connection between fear and puddles on the floor. And what would happen if we pushed him off the bridge and let him crash on the trafficway below?"

"He'd melt. Almost anything you'd do to him, he'd either melt, or he wouldn't do anything at all."

"Melting doesn't leave very convincing remains, does it, Greg?"

"Oh, they can analyze everything nowadays, mama, and tell just what it comes from. They get out their chemistry sets and analyze things with them."

"I suppose so. Well, let's get a lot of paper towels and spread them out here pretty thick. They should absorb the evidence as good as anything. Yes, that's fine. Get another roll, Greg, and spread them a little wider. Get two more rolls. We want to get every drop of him."

"All right," Greg said.

Then Petronilla brought Greatheart to the prepared place.

"How about the cloak and the tunic and the shako and the belts and the boots and the whip?" she asked Greg. "Could we save them?"

"No, I don't think so. They'll melt when he does."

Strega O'Conner came in from across the street. She always came in when something was going on.

"Well, this is the end of the episode, Greatheart," Petronilla said to her husband of three days. "But it isn't as though I hadn't arranged to have plenty to remember you by."

"Oh yes, I really must be getting back home," Greatheart

said. "If only I could escape from the sorceries I would go home now."

"I can help you to escape from the sorceries," Petronilla said. "I can send you home. I'm going to do it right now."

"I'm embarrassed," Greatheart told her. "I would like to give you a gift worthy of your kindness, but all I seem to possess at the moment is money."

"That will do nicely, Greatheart. Gregory, bring all the laundry baskets you can find, and we'll fill them up. Oh, that *is* pretty stuff, and you have so much of it, don't you? It was thoughtful of Gregory to give you the money trait and the glad-hand trait. Greg, press it down and the baskets will hold more. But that seems to be all that he has. The never-fail pockets have finally failed. But, after all, we aren't greedy, are we?"

"I am, kind of," Gregory said.

"All right, stand right here, Greatheart. I will break the sorceries and I will send you home."

"Will it hurt?" Greatheart Noble asked.

"I don't know," Petronilla admitted. "If you're not real, then I guess it won't really hurt."

Petronilla pulled one arm clear off Greatheart, and he began to collapse. Then the other arm and part of a shoulder came loose. His head fell off and rolled around on the floor. Then he melted completely. He made a pretty large puddle, but the piles of paper towels would soak up most of it.

Petronilla phoned the doctor and said that her husband had died in a household accident. She told the doctor to make out some sort of death certificate and to make it look good. Then she bundled up all the sopping paper towels and started over to the insurance office with them, to present the mortal remains of her husband and to collect the insurance on them.

3

Petronilla Ashling Noble was in chancery court on an insurance suit and countersuit, and things were going a little bit against her. She didn't have any lawyer. She said that after she had explained the simple facts of the case to three different lawyers, they had all walked away shaking their heads, and all of them had refused to represent her in the case.

"I understand how they felt," the chancery judge said. "I've been shaking my own head quite a bit. Are you sure that these two children have to be here?"

"Yes. I've told you that they are the two witnesses to the melting, ah, death of my husband Greatheart Noble," Petronilla said.

"Oh yes. But does the little girl have to be jumping rope all the time that court is going on?"

"Yes, she does," said Strega's mother Clementine O'Conner. "Whenever she has to stop jumping rope she has a tantrum."

"Sometimes one must make a choice," the judge said. "The tantrums, are they . . . ?"

"Yes, they're worse than the rope-jumping," Clementine said, and the judge sighed.

"I suggest again that this case be thrown out," the insurance-company representative said. "I maintain that there never was such a person as the insured Greatheart Noble."

"But you yourself talked to him," Petronilla argued, "and you yourself signed the receipt for the premium payments."

"I talked to a clown in some sort of costume," the insurance representative said. "It is clear fraud."

"I have proof of my marriage to Greatheart," Petronilla said. "I have proof of his appearance before the insurance people and of his physical examination. Why do all you people keep arguing with me? Pay me my money! I have proof of everything."

"Proof of everything except the husband's identity," the judge said, "and his death."

"Well, what in jug-headed judgment would you call proof?" Petronilla demanded.

"His mortal remains," the chancery judge said.

"Oh, you disgrace to the judiciary!" Petronilla squalled. "You *have* his mortal remains right in front of you on the bench!"

"I have here a horrific mess of old paper towels," the judge said. "They do not look like the mortal remains of a husband to me."

"You are supposed to have had those paper towels analyzed by experts to see what they soaked up."

"That has been done. And one of the experts is right here. And what the paper towels soaked up was water and nothing else. Or hardly anything else."

"What else? Tell me what else was found?" Petronilla demanded.

"As would be expected, there were small quantities of foreign matter."

"Oh, blindfolded justice! That foreign matter was my husband! Wheat bran and hog's blood, that's what the foreign matter was. That's what they made my husband out of."

"Oddly enough, the foreign matter *was* wheat bran and hog's blood," the expert said.

"Quiet!" the judge croaked. "I adjourn this court till I don't know when."

> "This is the plaintiff, this is the place,
> This is the judge all red in the face."

That was Strega O'Conner who had been singing a rope-jump song for quite a while and it had finally got under the subliminal skin of the judge.

There was some confusion along about then, and unreal elements seemed to creep in.

"You will *not* adjourn this court till you make them pay me my insurance money!" Petronilla said with such anger and violence that the judge seemed to go into a state of white-faced fear. "You will get back to that bench or I will drag you back," Petronilla swore. Petronilla had hold of the judge and she had him scared. He began to cave in and to shrink. He almost began to disintegrate. And was that not a small puddle that had formed on the floor, and was it not growing larger?

> "This is the puddle, thin as whey.
> A gentleman drowned in it today," Strega jump-sang.

Petronilla was attempting to drag the judge back to his place on the bench, and that shrinking judge was resisting.

Then (oh horror!) Petronilla pulled one arm clear off the judge—
And Strega was rope-jumping and rhyming—
And the head fell off and—

Chancery courts were very informal in those days. This condition has since been corrected.

HADES AND EUCLID

BY HARRY MARTINSON

translated by Robert Bly

I

When Euclid started out to measure Hades,
he found it had neither depth nor height.
Demons flatter than stingrays
swept above the plains of death,
their barks had no echoes as they ran
along the fire frontiers and the ice frontiers,
along the lines laid down in Hades.

Along the lines that fell apart
and joined again as lines
flock after flock of demons went abreast, in ranks, and
        parallel through Hades.

There were only waves, no hills, no chasms or valleys.
Only lines, parallel happenings, angles lying prone.
Demons shot along like elliptical plates;
they covered an endless field in Hades as though with
        moving dragonscales.

On the smoothed-over burial mounds that forgetfulness
        had destroyed with its flatness,

snakes were crawling—they were merely heavy lines:
lashed, crawled, stung their way
along the flowing lines.

A raging grassfire in roaring flatflight
rushed over the ground like a carpenter's plane of fire.
It shot over the evil prairies, over the evil steppes, over
          the flat evil pusta
back and forth, ignited again and again by heat
on the flat fields in Hades.

II

The ovens of Hell lay close to the ground
on the flat fields.
There the capriciously damned were burned
in the brick rooms—
near the surface as graves are—
victims of flat evil,
with no comfort from a high place
or support from a low place,
received without dignity,
received without a rising,
received without any of the standards of eternity.
Their cries are met only by mockery
on the flat fields of evil.

And Euclid, the king of measurement, cried
and his cry went looking for Kronus, the god of spheres.

For lo! the days are hast'ning on,
  By prophets seen of old,
When with the ever-circling years
  Shall come the time foretold. . . .

—Edmund Hamilton Sears,
"It Came Upon a Midnight Clear"

CHRISTMAS
IN WATSON HOLLOW

BY JERROLD MUNDIS

Everyone grows a little melancholy at Christmas time. Reflection is a natural consequence, and that's what I'm doing this evening of December 26, reflecting. Christmas, locally, is a small affair, as it must be in other places; we learn of its larger effect only in the newspapers and on television in the days after.

It visited us modestly here in Watson Hollow but was still of some character. Mae Sporky, for example, hanged herself in the belfry of the Presbyterian church. She'll be missed by her husband and children but not the town in general, since she was a busybody and caused embarrassment to many.

Each year on December 25, as the sun sets, God sends the Angel of Death winging down to earth with a sharpened scythe, which whistles through the air: *scrreeeeeeeeeee.* If your faith is deep, and you listen very hard, and have a little luck, you can hear it sometimes. The Angel of Death yearns for this night throughout all the 364 others. It is the one in which he finds his deepest fulfillment. Statistically, he reaps 25 percent of his annual harvest on Christmas night, or, as any schoolchild can tell you, a full one-quarter. The Angel is a serious, stylish, nasty, demented, and pranksterish spirit. Sometimes he does the work himself, leaping upon a sleeping schoolteacher and throttling her. Or he'll force self-destruction, as with Mae. On other occasions he might use a second party as agent upon the first: recall the wife of the mayor of Pittsburgh, who roasted her infant daughter and served her up with dumpling gravy last year.

We do not call these people who die victims but rather selections. "Selection" is a word without valuative judgment (other than that it is a thing chosen), whereas "victim" denotes some-

65

one of innocence who suffers because of ruthless design. And while the Angel of Death acts wholly upon his own whimsy, it is still God from whom his authority derives (as indeed does the authority for everything we can perceive). Thus, since God is incapable of ruthlessness, it would be error to think in terms of victims. In fact, it was this very concept of victim that spawned the Manerian Heresy in France, which ultimately resulted in the Hundred Years' War.

When the Angel of Death comes swooping down, he sings:

> "I'm gonna getcha, I'm gonna getcha,
> I'm gonna getcha, yes I am!"

We have this on the report of St. Helena of Damascus, who was struck down by the Angel on three successive Christmases but who had lived with such exceptional purity that her body, to the astonishment of neighbors and friends, suffered neither decay nor mortification and who was miraculously restored to life each Easter Sunday following her demise. St. Helena's favorite animal was the rabbit, and thus rose the legend of the Easter Bunny.

The Angel apparently works by mood or impulse. He might kill everyone in a family, or wipe out an entire street, or he might skip a city in total, a state, even a nation (though the latter has occurred infrequently in history). Sometimes he's gentle, and expiration eventuates with only a low sigh and a slump. Other times he'll burn you to death in a flaming gasoline explosion. Selection and mode of execution never correlate with the "goodness" or "badness" of an individual. Some unsophisticated minds see in this fact an arbitrariness on the part of God. But the more insightful will recognize in it yet another indication that He is ineffable, to say which, as Augustine reminds us, is already to have presumed too much.

Watson Hollow is a rural community, a town only by political definition. There are a little less than 600 people on the voter rolls. We have a stratum of elderly retired people, another of small businessmen who are the civic leaders, a handful of artists who have fled Manhattan, ridge runners or back mountain people, cautiously liberal management personnel from IBM, urban refugee families in which the man commutes back in to his job, and some just plain folks. It's a nice little town, American, community-minded, and we like it well enough.

The Angel took ten of us last night. Of course there's a fair amount of keeping to one's kind and, as you'd expect, not everyone knows everyone—but everyone does know someone, who knows someone else, who knows someone else. If it's a close strike you're informed in minutes; the last of the list comes trickling in by the time you've finished your morning coffee. Last year the Angel got my mother. She was up visiting with my stepfather over the holidays. The Angel blew her brain apart while she was standing at the washbasin in her nightgown. Spurted blood out her eyes and ears, got thick gobs of it all over the mirror and walls. We called the Watson Hollow First Aid Unit (not that there was anything that could be done, but we had to remove the body to a mortician) a little after midnight. The first sympathy call came in at 12:35 and the phone hardly stopped ringing after that.

This Christmas, Mae Sporky put on her galoshes and coat and told her family she was going out for some air. Eight minutes later the church sexton heard the bell tolling and found her bobbing slowly on the end of the rope. Mae's tracks led through the snow in a straight line from her house to the church door.

Jimmy Clark's red Corvair left the pavement on the switchback curve up on High Falls Road and he and Brenda Gilvey were flying at 70 miles per hour when they hit the concrete bridge abutment.

Harry Winchell, who drove a county grading machine and liked to throw people through bar windows, had the arteries and veins disconnected from his heart and he fell forward onto the kitchen table with his face in a bowl of ice cream.

The Angel wrenched off Frank Henderson's forearm at the elbow and beat him to death with it.

John VanGaasbeck and Sinclair Allen, two intellectuals retired from Columbia University, had met for their weekly night of discourse, which was at first spirited, then heated, and finally degenerated into name-calling while VanGaasbeck's wife clucked disapprovingly.

"Sophist!" VanGaasbeck cried.

"Kantian!" Allen retorted.

"Nihilist!"

"Panphysicist!"
"Casuist!"
"Dualist!"
"Fool!"
"Dunce!"
"Donkey!"

And at that point the Angel of Death rushed through the brick wall (visible only to the selection, as it should not be necessary to say) and climbed up on VanGaasbeck's back, threw a hand over his mouth and pinched his nostrils closed. VanGaasbeck shot from his chair and ran around the coffee table flailing his arms and kicking his knees high. He crashed to the floor and beat his head up and down, drummed his shoes, and made muffled sounds.

"Fakir!" Allen raged. "Swedenborgian, daemonicist, Thomist . . . asshole!"

On the other side of town a young woman making love to her husband was jerked out of bed, had her belly opened with a single swipe of the scythe, and her stomach was ripped out.

Little Tim Koeler's blood froze in his vessels while his twin brother Tom slept on beside him.

Pearl Bell, born and raised here, ninety-three years old and having at the disposal of her clear mind nearly 200 years of local history, a sprightly woman to whom graduate students and historians made weekly treks and who wouldn't speak a word until she was kissed on the mouth, was lifted several feet from the floor and squashed and twisted until her bones were broken and her organs ruptured.

The owner of the Watson Hollow Inn keeled over in the middle of a Republican dinner party. Medical examination could provide no explanation of the mode of his demise. He was just dead.

We came through better than some years, worse than others. Perhaps the only principle that can be drawn is that we came through.

This has been true since the night of that first Christmas, 3,000 years ago, when God in his anger sent down the Angel of Death to slay all the brown-eyed people in the city of Gath. God speaks so softly that we can hardly ever hear, but the stick he carries is large indeed, as we were given pause to contemplate

POETRY

Highway Sandwiches [with Charles Platt and Marilyn Hacker] (1970)
The Right Way to Figure Plumbing (1972)
ABCDEFG HIJKLM NPOQRST UVWXYZ (1981)
Burn This (1982)
Orders of the Retina (1982)
Here I Am, There You Are, Where Were We (1984)
Yes, Let's: New and Selected Poems (1989)
Dark Verses and Light (1991)
Haikus of an AmPart (1991)
The Dark Old House (1996)

AS EDITOR

Alfred Hitchcock's Stories That Scared Even Me [with Robert Arthur] (1967)
The Ruins of the Earth: An Anthology of Stories of the Immediate Future (1971)
Bad Moon Rising (1973)
New Constellations: An Anthology of Tomorrow's Mythologies (1976)
Strangeness: A Collection of Curious Tales (1977)

IF YOU'RE INTERESTED IN
ANY OF THESE BOOKS I HAVE
COPIES OF MANY OF THEM.
I LIVE IN THE NORTH END
NEIGHBORHOOD OF ST. PAUL.
THEY ARE FREE OF CHARGE

JEFF DISCH
charjeff@ q.com

Books by Thomas M. Disch

FICTION

The Genocides (1965)

Mankind Under the Leash (1966)

One Hundred and Two H-Bombs (1966)

Echo Round His Bones (1967)

Camp Concentration (1968)

Under Compulsion (1968)

The Prisoner (1969)

Getting Into Death and Other Stories (1973)

334 (1974)

The Early Science Fiction Stories of Thomas M. Disch (1977)

On Wings of Song (1979)

Fundamental Disch (1980)

Neighboring Lives [with Charles Naylor] (1981)

The Man Who Had No Idea (1982)

The Businessman: A Tale of Terror (1984)

The Brave Little Toaster (1986)

The Brave Little Toaster Goes to Mars (1988)

The M.D.: A Horror Story (1992)

The Priest: A Gothic Romance (1995)

The Word of God (2008)

The Wall of America [forthcoming] (Tachyon, 2008)

NON-FICTION

The Castle of Indolence: On Poetry, Poets, and Poetasters (1995)

The Dreams Our Stuff Is Made of: How Science Fiction Conquered the World
    (1998)

The Castle of Perseverance: Job Opportunities in Contemporary Poetry (2002)

On SF (2005)

again last night here in Watson Hollow, and as all men were across the world. The Angel takes wing each Christmas, and though individuals do not, man himself always comes through. And that is why we gather with friends and loved ones the night of Christmas After to exchange gifts beneath our Christmas trees, where, above the tinsel and ornaments, the candy canes and twinkling lights, on the very crown, a little figurine of the Angel of Death smiles down upon us.

IN A LAND
OF CLEAR COLORS

BY ROBERT SHECKLEY

> In a land of clear colors and stories,
>   In a region of shadowless hours,
> Where earth has a garment of glories
>   And a murmur of musical flowers;
> In woods where the spring half uncovers
>   The flush of her amorous face,
> By the waters that listen for lovers,
>   For these is there place?
>
> —Swinburne

The forms of things bear their own particular message. Here on Kaldor V there is an unsettling irrationality about many artifacts. That mountain in the distance—Ungdoor I think they call it—why should it look like a pyramid point down? Or take this forest—some of the trees are ten feet in diameter. Why should they all lie flat upon the ground? Or those birds, the Maagpi, who build their nests upon the air and who work in relays to support its weight? Why do the clouds regularly form themselves into arches?

These are only the more evident mysteries. And each mystery has a mystery hidden within it. I suppose they are all rationally explicable, even predictable. But not by me.

What worries me most just at the moment is this: Why do mirrors on Kaldor V never reflect back what looks into them?

In some ways my position is ridiculous. Thanks to mechanohypnosis, I can speak three of the major languages on Kal-

71

dor. But my sense of nuance is completely off. (I have the same trouble in speaking Spanish.)

We Terrans tend to believe that language is always intentional, that sentences are equations denoting operations, orders, sensations; that words mean what they say. But this is untrue, even on Earth and especially here on Kaldor. Words are intentional here also; but they tend to be used for other purposes.

Words are used with extreme indirection. To them, I suppose it's all very logical and inevitable. It is not impossible to extract the meaning from most exchanges. What is tedious is the work involved. Because this great effort must be made with everything; nothing comes easy, nothing can be taken for granted.

This must explain the high rate of emotional malfunction among Interactors.

The problems of extraterrestrial exploration are always the same. First problem, how to stay alive. Second (close on its heels), how to stay sane. The uncertainty tends to be maximized. The biggest danger on an alien planet might well be anxiety.

Culture shock is the problem. An overload of novelty is insupportable. One tends to blank out, to stop registering, or to do so in a hasty, inattentive manner.

Decision-making is also affected—disastrously. There are too many imponderables to be weighed, too many courses of action to be chosen among, and always on the basis of insufficient information.

A paralysis of the will sets in. One reaches a point where you can't decide whether to make fried eggs or boiled eggs. Everything must stop while this decision is being made. And when it has been made, one is too exhausted to eat.

I used to think that exploring an alien planet would be like seeing a very strange movie. I was prepared for that; but I had not counted on the fact that I would be a participant, not a spectator.

Lanea came by today to see how I was getting on. Or at least I presume that is why she came. I find her presence both disturbing and comforting. I have grown accustomed to her anatomical differences. Her extreme physical flexibility (a trait she shares with most other Kaldorians) is still a wonder to me. The appearance is one of bonelessness, especially in arms, legs, neck. She can turn her head a full 180 degrees and look directly behind her. I have asked her not to do this in my presence.

I have every reason to believe—though I have not yet verified it—that her sexual structures, concealed under her clothing, are similar to those of a Terran woman.

Will I ever find this out by actual experience? I should not be thinking such thoughts.

Her face is a long oval, delicately proportioned, beautiful by Earth standards. She has a faint Eurasian look; but, ironically enough, she would not be considered "exotic" on Earth. She could pass unnoticed in a crowd on Earth. Except for her walk, of course, which is sinuous, flowing, faintly repelling, faintly exciting.

Her appearance doesn't bother me. Quite the contrary. But her mind . . .

One cannot expect to understand any woman, I suppose. But what is one to do about an alien woman?

Nothing, of course! Anyhow, what would Lanea want with me? In her eyes I must be a freak, both in appearance and mentality.

Doerniche is in his fifties (apparently), a lean, spare man of great dignity, a holder of a seat on the Council. He came here today and tried to warn me about something. I do not know what it is. Despite my best efforts, and his, I could not make it out. He seems to have no specific danger in mind; yet I cannot believe that a man of Doerniche's intelligence would waste his time and effort on a general statement about the danger of the world.

I have seen no hint of danger. What can he be talking about?

Doerniche is so ornate—might he not be talking about something else entirely? It wouldn't be the first time that has happened. It is one of the vices of this language. If you miss one of the key words or inflections, the meaning is altered drastically. Sentences begun with a certain combination of vowels, for example, are not meant to be taken literally. Their purpose is obliquely metaphoric.

So I may have missed a subtlety in Doerniche's speech. God knows what else I've missed and what wrong assumptions I am operating on here.

Still, I wish I knew whether or not there is a specific danger to me.

I live in a small white house some four or five miles from the outer periphery of Morei. The government constructed this house for me when they saw that I was ill at ease in the city. They built it like an Earth house, copied from one of the pictures I had brought along. I did not ask for this; they did it of their own accord, to surprise and please me.

At first, I considered it a dubious compliment. I wondered if they were not attempting, with infinite politeness, to exile me, to insulate me in my alienness.

But now I do not think this was the intention. They know about homesickness in this place; many of their songs and stories are about that.

So they built me a house that looks exactly like a New England bungalow—until you study the shapes and angles with more care. Then it looks like nothing under the sun.

I've grown accustomed to it.

I began to understand the conversation of the flowers last night.

One must listen to them with great attentiveness. Their voices are soft (as you would expect) and tend to a monotone. They cannot pronounce d's, t's, r's. They express various fine meanings by modulating volume. They make an intensive use of silence (stops and rests, as in music) to cover an additional range of meanings, as do the Kaldorians. How they produce their sounds I do not know, nor care to know. I know too much already.

I hereby translate and transcribe the following conversation, held in my garden just two hours ago, between something that looked like a rose and something that looked like an azalea.

ROSE: How are you today?
AZALEA: Very well, thank you. And you?
ROSE: Well enough. If only it would rain!

AZALEA: Rain would be welcome. I love rain.

ROSE: I do, too. Especially soft rains.

AZALEA: Oh, they are by far the nicest. Especially when they come with just a little south wind.

ROSE: By all means, the south wind completes it. How I love rain!

AZALEA: And I, too. I am going to rest now.

ROSE: It has been very nice talking to you again.

AZALEA: I enjoyed it very much. Thank you, and grow in good health.

ROSE: May your leaves spread! Goodbye!

AZALEA: Goodbye!

That is what they said, verbatim. What inferences should be drawn from this? At one time I would have jumped to the conclusion that flowers tend to be sweet, simple-minded, prolix. Now, I simply don't know. Was their talk as banal as it seemed to me? Or might those two have been making love with words?

This planet is bulging with phenomena. But I don't know what any of it means. And the longer I stay here, the less I know.

I was a volunteer in the First Extraterrestrial Exploration Corps. We were all very young and idealistic. I could conceive of nothing more noble and important than the task of exploring the planets, establishing contact with other intelligences, working toward a great harmony and cooperation.

Now I can take that sort of thing or leave it. But then I was a zealot. I passed all of the tests, and I was among the first thousand to go E.T.

Our ships were small. They were not places in which to live; they were cocoons in which to hibernate. We were scattered into space like seeds cast to the winds.

Well, we weren't exactly scattered; we were *aimed,* more or less. The ships were constructed to home on various selected planet-bearing stars, to examine those planets for various criteria, to awaken the explorer if the planet proved viable, and then to land. Or to leave him in hibernation and travel on to an alternate target if the planet were unsuitable.

Optimists thought that half of us might live to see an alien world, if we were extremely lucky.

Their predictions didn't matter to us. We considered this work a crusade.

Twenty ships were keyed to Kaldor V. Mine seems to be the only one that made it.

Why me? Why not any of the others? Were they killed in space, the other nineteen? Then how did I come to arrive without incident, according to the ship's automatic log? This seems to me statistically improbable.

It seems more likely that some of the others did arrive, that they are in other parts of Kaldor, that they have remained hidden; or, more likely, the authorities have either killed them or kept them incommunicado, without knowledge of each other.

I don't know what they are going to do with me. Doerniche speaks of danger, and I am beginning to believe him.

Someone came in the night and left a present on my doorstep. It is a figurine, about six inches high, carved of some lustrous red stone. The lines of the carving are exquisite. The piece is highly stylized; I cannot tell whether it is meant to be male, female, or neuter. The figure's feet are hidden in silvery metallic threads.

I shall put this in a place of honor on my mantel. I wish I knew who gave it to me. Doerniche? Lanea? I don't believe that either of them would leave presents anonymously in the night. Whoever gave it to me, my heart is warmed. I shall consider it my Christmas present from Kaldor V.

Doerniche came again today with three other members of the Council. They harangued me for about three hours. They were all dressed in their ceremonial robes, I suppose to underline the seriousness of the occasion. It was hard to take them seriously; the three who accompanied Doerniche might have been selected to exemplify the basic somatotypes. Grandinang was a roly-poly endomorph, nearly bald, choleric, incoherent in his exasperation. Pan Wolfing was the mesomorph, a powerful man of medium height, blunt-featured, self-possessed, courteous, with an athlete's unconscious grace even in his smallest gestures. And Eliaming was the ectomorph, skinny and intellectual, brilliant and erratic, ancient and boyish at the same time.

The four of them had come, I believe, to make me understand the danger I was in, something about nightwinds, and to make that danger evident to me despite language difficulties. They supplemented each other's explanations, interrupted each other to clarify various points, introduced a historical background, argued about the import of various recent events concerning me. The result was chaotic, disturbing to all of us, uninformative, and not at all helpful.

Doerniche came by, stayed only a moment, asked me to attend an important ceremony or holiday in the city in three days. It seems to be more than a casual invitation, so I shall attend. It begins at dawn tomorrow.

There was a stiff breeze last night, the first I can remember in some weeks. Might not that be the nightwind they have been referring to?

Lanea said she would come this morning. It is noon and she still has not arrived. I could use the inter-city communications net and speak to her. But I don't really understand how the net works.

Or I could go and see her. But she lives in the inner city, a labyrinth of tiny streets (like the Casbah of Algiers). I would probably get lost. Besides, I don't feel capable of that much initiative, even though I want to see her very much.

In the early afternoon I listened again to the flowers. (How mad that sounds!) I can understand them better than the Kaldorians. Their language structure is simpler. Flowers don't say much that is meaningful, but at least I can comprehend them. Which just may prove that my understanding is on a vegetative level.

This time they had something to say apart from their usual banalities. I repeat the talk verbatim, using Terran equivalents for the various species:

AZALEA TO ROSE: My dear, how well you look today!
ROSE: Do you think so? I feel wretched.
AZALEA: You look unbelievably young. What has happened?
ROSE: Well, it is almost time for my *farqhar*. (This seems to

be referring to some important physiological change.) That is upsetting.

AZALEA: But exhilarating!

ROSE (despondently): I suppose so. But I have been so happy in this garden.

AZALEA: You can come back any time you want.

ROSE: Nobody comes back. Remember lilac? She swore that she would come back at least once, she promised to tell us what it was like.

AZALEA: She still may come.

ROSE: No, she won't. She would if she were able, but I know that she cannot.

SYCAMORE (interrupting, speaking in a curiously high-pitched voice): Hey!

ROSE: Were you addressing me?

SYCAMORE: Yes, you. Scared of *farqhar,* are you?

ROSE: Of course, aren't you?

SYCAMORE: Not at all. I have faith.

ROSE: Faith in what?

SYCAMORE: I am an adept of the cult of Nimosim, who is the spirit dwelling in all rooted things.

AZALEA (crossly): And what does your faith teach you?

SYCAMORE: We of the Nimosim believe that there is a divine spirit in all vegetation. We believe that after *farqhar* we go to a place called Lii, where the ground is transparent, the wind blows forever from the south, and there are no rats to destroy our roots. There are streams of crystal water in this place, nourishing water that never is capable of rotting our leaves. In Lii we are granted the gift of infinite growth without ever overcrowding our neighbors. There is much more, but I can reveal the rest only to an adept.

ROSE: How beautiful your religion is!

AZALEA: What nonsense! After *farqhar,* you will become kindling wood, nothing more.

SYCAMORE: And my spirit?

AZALEA: It will perish with you, it will be obliterated, never to exist again.

ROSE: That's a terrible thing to say!

AZALEA: The truth may not be pleasant but is still the truth.

SYCAMORE: You do not possess the truth. Your method is to

think the worst possible, and then to speak it, hoping that it will not happen. But that is merely the voice of your fear, nothing else.

AZALEA: I could tell you more, but I think we are being overheard.

ROSE: How is that possible? We are quite alone here.

AZALEA: Not alone. There is an animal quite close to us.

SYCAMORE (bursting into high-pitched laughter): But animals don't understand us! They can't even understand each other! It is well known that animals cannot possess intelligence.

AZALEA: I am not so sure. This particular animal—

ROSE: One animal is like another animal!

AZALEA: I'm not at all sure about that. I would prefer to wait until he has gone.

ROSE: Superstitious!

AZALEA: My dear, I don't believe in intelligent animals, but I fear them. Yes, and I feel sorry for them.

SYCAMORE: Why?

AZALEA: For many reasons. But most of all because of the troubles they will soon experience.

ROSE: Animals can't feel pain!

AZALEA: Probably not. But suppose they could . . .

ROSE (soberly): Yes, that would be terrible. Soon the night-winds will be blowing, and the world will end.

AZALEA: Now, then! It's not as bad as that!

ROSE: It's bad enough. I shall sleep now. Good night.

AZALEA: Good night.

SYCAMORE: Good night and thank you for a lovely party.

So even among the flowers there are atheists and believers. It is all rather astounding. Unless, of course, I have imagined the whole thing.

That would still be astounding. But in a different and more ominous way.

I ate lunch and Lanea still had not come. I lay down on the sofa and fell asleep. I had the following dream:

I was walking down a twisty cobblestoned street in an ancient village. Two people came from the left and approached me. I started to ask them a question. They seemed afraid of me; they turned and ran. I ran after them, wishing to reassure them of my good intentions. But they would not listen to me, they ran faster, outdistancing me. Then I reached the center of the village, and there was a great bonfire in the plaza, and it rose higher, higher than the church. But I felt no heat.

Then I woke up, shaking, frightened, cold with sweat. Lanea came just a moment after that.

Actually, it has all worked out well. It's worked out marvelously. I don't know what I was so eternally upset for. Rereading my own notes, I am astounded. They seem literally the work of a different man. I suppose I should examine them more closely, try to figure out what was wrong with me. But I have no time these days. I am forever and constantly preoccupied.

The role of seer was not of my choosing. Yet that seems to be what I have become to them. I don't agree with the judgment, I must hasten to say. The fact that I have crossed empty space is not *prima facie* evidence of my superiority. Yet they don't see it that way.

There is no public acknowledgment of this, of course, nothing in the newspapers or on the radio. No, it is simply visible in the way people act toward me.

There is a great deal of work to be done around here and not much time to do it in. I am organizing things to the best of my abilities, but there is still a great deal I don't know. I am an alien, after all.

The west wall is particularly a problem, and I have been concentrating my efforts there. You see, the oncoming force will strike first at this wall. Therefore, it should be proportionally stronger than the others. But it is not.

We shore it up with masonry, cement, brick. It has to withstand that first monstrous shock of the nightwinds.

Now I do wish to make this clear—the nightwinds are true winds and could easily avoid the west wall if they wished. But they do not so wish. Their desire is not merely to rule; it is to exemplify. Therefore they accept the notion of a contest with rules and acknowledge themselves defeated if that rule is flouted.

The rule: They must breach the walls to win. If the walls

hold them out, then they have lost.

I build many layers. Everyone agrees that this is the best system. Lanea, my wife, has publicly looked upon them and held silence. This is an honor rarely won.

Aside from that, I have lived a normal life. I take pride in my collection of nail-parings, which experts say compares favorably with that of the Hidden Ruler. I still need therapy now and then for obsession removal. (In that I am much like everyone else.)

Lanea is good enough to allow me to be of considerable service to her. It is a mark of her love that I may wash her feet every night. Not only that, but she has allowed me to expect it, without being tantalized every day as to its possibility. She has been good in other ways, too. She held my hand throughout the mutilation ceremony, and it really didn't hurt as much as I had feared. She has humiliated me in front of her peers. Even her parents have come to despise me—I had not expected so much.

I suppose that she loves me so because I am an alien from Earth and therefore despicable. But I don't care about that any more. I am quite happy being despicable, especially with such a wife as Lanea to help me.

I don't suppose I can hope to hold her love for long. Men never do. I suppose I will be sold like all the others to the public whorehouses, where I will lead a loveless and irritated life. Or perhaps something else will happen, perhaps banishment, perhaps impalement. Or a lighter destiny? We men have our folklore, too.

In the meantime, I do what is necessary. I pile up bricks, using my tail as a counterweight rather than as a third hand. I hammer cement into place with my forehead. I extend my nose into the air, trying to sniff out the first approach of the wind of change.

And the important thing is this: I am happy, I am marvelously happy. I suppose that stating that is superfluous. I suppose that anyone reading this account could tell how happy I was. Yet I feel the need to repeat it, not obsessionally but rather as a hymn, a paean.

I am still in contact, you see. I know that I am an Earthman, I know that I am on an alien planet. But I also know what I have become, which is completely and marvelously a Kaldorian.

I want to note all of this down to remind myself, in case I should happen to forget.

I have reread my own notes, I am reminded, and I am horribly afraid.

What in God's name came over me?

Why did I write that infernal drivel?

I am sitting in my house on Kaldor. It is a bright day. I am sitting in the rocking chair. My hands seem steady. I can hear a whistle from the teapot in the kitchen. (They have teapots on Kaldor but not tea.) I see dust motes in the rug, and I see the windows, small, dusty, glittering with light. On the mantel is a red statuette. I remember that, too, and I am still afraid.

I would like to sort this out. Something must have happened to me over the last week, which is the length of time my last notes cover. Something must have happened, because that much time did indeed pass. I must have been somewhere—here in my house, perhaps, asleep or in a coma. Or perhaps I was that person I described with so much glee, that cheerful masochistic moron.

Lanea was by earlier. She brought a can of jelly which her grandmother made. The jelly here is quite good. I had some of it on crackers (they have crackers on Kaldor) and I spoke to her about the last week.

She looked away from me; she would not meet my eyes. She said, "It is better not to think of such things."

"I bloody well know that," I told her. "I simply want to know if it happened. Did I in fact turn into some sort of a creature with a tail?"

"You are brooding," Lanea said, "and that is bad for anyone. Will you go for a walk with me today?"

"First answer my question," I said.

She twisted her hands together in that supple, ugly gesture. She turned her face away. After a moment I noticed that her shoulders were shaking, and I knew that she was crying.

I went over and tried to comfort her, but she turned furiously and said, "You are an alien and that excuses very much, but sometimes your behavior is not suitable for any intelligent being!"

I tried to hold her, but she pushed past me and rushed out the door. I heard her footsteps on the street and I did not try to follow her.

I sat quite alone in my armchair trying to sort things out, and after a while Grandinang came by and I told him what had happened.

"Women are that way," he assured me. "They shrink from so-called vulgarities, though they are ever ready to act them out."

"But what vulgarity was she shrinking from?"

Grandinang looked not precisely embarrassed, more puzzled and apprehensive. Then he said, "Goldstein, it just occurred to me that you cannot be conversant with all our ways. To us, it is perfectly natural to avoid any mention of the first Alternate. The women are especially nervous. And even most of us men, to tell you the truth, would prefer to forget about the whole thing."

I wanted to forget about it, too; but I was afraid that my sanity was at stake. I had to know what had happened.

Grandinang was not about to give me a straight answer at this stage of the game, and he knew it. But he handled it nicely. He said, "I could give you my view of it, of course, but that would be biased. I think it would be best if you looked it up in the archives. The full account of everything, or almost everything, is there. The language is a bit archaic at times, but you manage so well—"

I thanked him, and he got up to go. I asked, "Will you see Lanea soon?"

"Not sooner than you."

"Why is that?"

"Why, good God, man, she *is* your wife."

And then, as if he realized he had said too much, he went quickly out the door.

This evening Lanea returned. She has been here almost an hour and we haven't yet exchanged a word. She is in the kitchen, preparing our dinner. I believe Grandinang, I believe that she is my wife. I can't imagine—or remember—how this came about, but I know that it is so.

I find her desirable, repellent. I do not love her. I do want her. But I do not *want* to want her.

That leaves me in a clumsy position, engaged in combat with myself.

It is all too much. I am finding it difficult to believe that there is a place called Earth, that I left that place in some sort of a contrivance, that I came here, talked with flowers, degraded myself, married Lanea. It is all too much.

Lanea is calling me to come eat dinner. The ugly thought just struck me. She prepared food for me, but what does she eat herself? Does she eat me?

That is unworthy of me and unfair to Lanea. Nevertheless, I go to the table now with a certain apprehension.

Lanea is very beautiful and loving. That is some compensation for the steady attrition of my humanity.

We play a pretty domestic scene, Lanea and I. She brings me breakfast, walking briskly into the bedroom in her swirling morning coat. I drink a warm, mild stimulant, about the equivalent of coffee. I am the only person on Kaldor who does this. Little habits like that help me to remember who I am.

Then I work on my notes, slides, tapes. After lunch I go for a walk. Usually I turn away from the city, into stubbled fields and second-growth forest. I take along a flute that Wolfing made for me. Its tones are not quite true, but I don't mind; my own tones are not quite true either.

There is a hill several miles from here called Nmassi. I usually climb it and sit on its pointed top all alone, playing my flute and resting my eyes on distant scenery. I play "When You're a Long, Long Way from Home" and "Amapola" and "Flying Down to Rio" and other songs that are all but forgotten even on Earth. The songs sound strange in this place; the notes are a miniature invasion, bravely piped, soon lost in the immensities of Kaldor. While playing, I am a Terran. But at night, in Lanea's arms, I do not know what I am.

Not a Kaldorian by any means. But not quite human either. A changeling, perhaps.

Lanea knows with her own wisdom who and what I am. Sometimes she holds me very tight, as if I might fly off into the vacuum of space. Sometimes she holds my face in her two hands, looks into my eyes, and makes a strange sound deep in her throat. Sometimes she squeezes my hand, tight, tight.

I do not think I will ever be rescued. I will live out my time here. And if there is a heaven or hell, it will be a Kaldorian one to which I will be consigned. Or perhaps there is a special limbo for those who have severed their roots, who are no longer of one stock, not yet of another.

In the meantime, I have no real complaints.

Having taken a wife, or been taken by one, I suppose I could not avoid the problem of in-laws. I wouldn't be surprised to find that a universal constant. These are not quite what you would expect, however: Lanea's parents change every week.

So far I have counted three sets of parents.

Their behavior with me is similar enough to consider them a single set.

Nevertheless, there are three (so far).

I have questioned Lanea about this. She finds it strange and funny that I ask. She laughs at me—and her laugh is beautiful. She says, "How do you manage it on Earth, then?"

"With one father and one mother," I tell her. "Of course, in the past, some Terran societies had variations on the theme—extended families, for one, or passing on the paternal or maternal role to an uncle or aunt."

"How complicated!" she says. "Why not simply start right off with a parental group?"

"I don't know," I tell her. "It simply happened that way." (How quickly I become defensive about the customs of Earth.)

"Here," she said, "we cooperate in vital functions. We have a saying, you know—the more parents the better."

"I've heard the saying," I tell her. "But which of the parents physically gave birth to you?"

She shakes her head reprovingly. "I do not know that myself. That is a mystery."

"Why don't you ask?"

"Because I don't want to know. There would no longer be a mystery, then."

"Is it so important to have a mystery?"

"Oh, yes." She looked at me very seriously, eyes wide and intent. "We of Kaldor have many mysteries. Mystery of one sort or another is the core of our existence."

"On Earth," I told her, "we explore mysteries and try to explain how they work."

She nodded gravely. "That is because you are a passionate and impatient people; you solve smaller mysteries in order to find others that are beyond your understanding."

"How can you possibly know that?"

"Because you are here on Kaldor, having gambled your life against great odds to cross the mystery of space and find the strangeness of another race. Your journey here was like an initiation ceremony, like our Time of Destruction. But we of Kaldor would not do this. We have enough mysteries on our own planet without the need to cross space in order to find more."

I push on in my blunt, uncomprehending way. "What is the reason for having three sets of parents?"

"We don't have three sets; we usually have four."

"Then I haven't met one of your fathers and mothers."

"Nor have I. One parental group is never revealed except under certain special conditions."

"Why?"

"There are reasons. But above all, it is another mystery."

"You seem to have a lot of mysteries," I comment.

"Oh, yes! It is the key to understanding us."

I realize that this is true. A month ago I would have plunged on, asked her to state exactly what a mystery was, if it was an invention or a discovery, how many mysteries they possessed, which were the most characteristic, and so forth. Now I am no less curious, but I have learned a little of the usages of this place. There are things that one simply does not ask. Not outright. I hope to find out more about this matter, but I will have to suit my inquiries to local conditions.

And then Lanea is sitting in my lap, her arms around my neck, her lips pressed against my face. Gently I stroke her long dark hair. She sighs, her arms tighten, she adjusts herself to fit my body more closely.

Perhaps women are similar all over the universe?

It surprises me now that I could ever eat meat. Here on Kaldor the taboo against meat runs very deeply and is comparable to our own revulsion against cannibalism. I share the Kaldorian meat phobia now; I suppose I learned it by empathy from Lanea, my in-laws, and the population at large.

It occurs to me now that I did eat meat when I first came here; that Doerniche and others supplied it. I can't remember whether they ate with me, but it seems entirely possible. More likely, they disguised a vegetarian dish to simulate meat. Their better chefs have more than enough skill to do this. Mock-meat is ceremonially served on one occasion in the year.

The Kaldorians are most notable, in my estimation, for their sense of the wholeness and interrelatedness of life. They seem to have an innate ecological sense, which runs in them as deep and true as the sex drive. The Kaldorian, although conscious of a unique status by virtue of his intelligence, still views himself as an animal living in a natural habitat. He changes his environment, but so do beavers. In each case, the changes wrought are relatively minimal and predictable.

Most of this planet is wilderness, despite the fact that civilized and mobile races have occupied it for thousands of years. This knowledge gives me an indescribable sense of peace and freedom.

The Kaldorian food taboo does not limit itself only to meat, fish and fowl, and their products. The taboo extends also to many vegetables.

This, in my opinion, is not illogical. When you think about it, why should animal status be the main criterion of who or what gets eaten? Is not a carrot worthy of life, despite the fact that it might lack mobility?

It is not very logical to look over the attributes you possess and then declare that they are the most important attributes in the universe.

How could I eat that talking rose, azalea, and sycamore in my backyard?

How could I eat any creature that talked, whether it was animal or vegetable?

Suppose the steak on your table cried out to you for help? What if the veal cutlet begged you to restore it to its mother? Suppose beans screamed when they were being boiled?

This is how the Kaldorians feel, and I concur. This attitude leaves them with a problem. What are they going to eat?

I am afraid they have solved the problem only through hypocrisy. They have designated certain plants that may be eaten. All others are forbidden.

Still, I may be wrong about hypocrisy. I questioned Wolfing about this once. He insisted that certain plants were permissible food through essence, not through arbitrary choice.

"How are they different from other plants?" I asked.

He looked at me strangely, and I knew that once again I was asking questions that should not be asked. Any Kaldorian would understand the answer without its ever having been stated. But Wolfing was very good about realizing that I had not been born here.

Wolfing said at last, "Those plants do not dream."

I didn't know what to make of this answer. I asked him to tell me more of the differences.

"Those plants do not change like the others," he said.

"Change? Do you mean blossom?"

He shook his head impatiently. "When I say they do not change, I mean they retain their constancy by day, week, month and year."

"Are they immortal?"

"Perhaps, in some special sense. But in a special sense we all are."

"Yes . . . Is there anything else about them?"

"Those plants do not *feel* right. It is very difficult to describe," Wolfing said. "The impression is qualitatively different. I suppose you might call them inert. By which I do not mean dead. Nor do I mean to imply a value judgment. I simply mean that they feel different from all other plants."

Wolfing was talking with animation now; his words poured out easily.

"But we do not know what the difference means. Perhaps the permissible plants are recent arrivals, seeds or spores from meteorites and other cosmic debris. Perhaps they have not become fully a part of this planet. Or perhaps the opposite is true, perhaps they are the oldest inhabitants, perhaps they have evolved beyond our comprehension. We simply don't know. We still do not like to eat them. But we do so in order to live and in accordance with the rule of like choosing unlike."

We looked at each other in that moment of full understanding that the Kaldorians call *d'bnai*. I was in full agreement, intellectually, with the Kaldorian concept of the sacredness of life. Earthmen's ideals state what they would like to become; Kaldor in that sense has no ideals. It has already become what it desired.

Yesterday was Sarameish, a very special holiday. Lanea and I were lucky enough to obtain first-row seats in the drawing.

Wolfing had also drawn a front-row seat, which pleased Lanea and myself very much. It meant that three of our friendship-bond had been lucky today, and thus we give our luck to the others.

I looked around to see where my friends were seated. Eliaming was in a fourth row behind a pillar. He smiled his pleasure at our good luck. Grandinang, the lovable fool, had contrived a part for himself in the ceremony—quite superfluously, since the Council Eyes would have picked him anyhow. And dear Doerniche was playing inger to the girls in the procession, as he had for the last three years since reaching his fullness.

Lanea and I were excited enough to hold hands. We clutched each other, waiting, scarcely breathing, even though the ceremony is almost the same year in and year out. Still, no one can contain himself on Sarameish.

Then the procession began. First the young girls, clothed all in white, and then the boys, in russet and forest green. Their dance was the utmost expression of a prayer.

Next, the God of Discord was brought in on his iron cart. (This is all symbolic, of course; no one believes in a literal God of Discord. They are addressing themselves to the attitude.)

The God was very splendid this year, almost ten feet tall, very portly, brilliantly colored in metallic blacks, reds, yellows. He looked impossibly solid and strong, invincible, in fact, and there were whispers of consternation throughout the stands; for the Artificer's Cooperative has been known to be overzealous at several points in their long history, making durable out of pride of craft what had been intended for a single day only.

The car comes to a stop. There are various propitiatory dances, several songs, a dramatic recitative. All of this is intoxicating; the finest expressions of theatrical arts are saved for this day.

All too soon that part is over. Then Doerniche steps forward.

He approaches the God with deliberate steps, and Lanea and I can hardly control ourselves for pride and joy that this man is in our friendship group. Doerniche stalks the God with slow steps, and some of the children start to cry. But Grandinang and the other clowns come out, dressed as flowers and herbivorous animals. They make jokes, sing nonsense songs, scramble under each other's legs and over each other's backs. The children scream with laughter, and even we adults must smile at the antics.

But our attention is abruptly diverted. Doerniche has reached the God; he has mounted the iron cart! Now, literally, we cannot see the clowns. All of our attention is focused on Doerniche, yes, and all-out concern.

Doerniche inspects the God and turns his back on him. We applaud. He turns again, takes a piece of the God's coat, and rips it off.

We fall silent, barely breathing.

With measured movements Doerniche rips off all the God's clothes, rendering him naked. We wait. Doerniche is committed now; he can no longer refuse the job. In his two bare hands the luck of the city resides.

He inspects the body of the God, which is made of various metals and looks as if it could withstand the eruption of a volcano. He touches this part and that, learning the nature of the ultimate evil he is encountering. His fingers glide over the God's face, down his massive chest, down his hard-muscled flanks . . .

Doerniche stops; he has found what he was looking for. He lunges suddenly at precisely the right spot. His hand penetrates the thin, soft sheet of copper, and his fingers rip upward, stopping only when they encounter bronze.

Doerniche's eyes are rolled blindly upward. He explores the hole he has made with his fingers. He probes, finds softness, rips, moves his hand, rips again, reaches inside the God, rips. He takes his hand out, there is blood on it, he reaches in again, his hand grips, he sets his feet, the cords in his neck stand out, he heaves. We in the stands hold our breath, and some of us have already begun to curse the Artificers, for we are afraid they have ruined the ceremony.

But then Doerniche relaxes; he has pulled something loose

within the God, and he takes it out and shows it to us: an iron stanchion, one of the internal supporting members. He holds it above his head and we applaud and hug each other with relief. (It is the same every year, and the stanchion always comes free, and Doerniche makes his muscles stand out for show but in reality he only must exert a moderate pull, and we know all of this, know that there is no reasonable way the ceremony can fail, nevertheless we are in anxiety until it actually happens. That is always how Sarameish affects us.)

With the iron bar removed, the God's left arm collapses onto the iron cart. The children shriek. Doerniche works quickly now, ripping copper and tearing out the God's supporting members, which we refer to as his ribs. Doerniche's movements become a dance which is accompanied by the slow, steady collapse of Discord. At last he reaches in and plucks out the spine and then steps nimbly out of the way. What was left of the God collapses in on itself. Doerniche reaches into the debris and plucks out a double-chambered globe of red quartz. This he shatters on the ground.

Now at last we can applaud, and we do so, releasing our tensions tumultuously. There are some hours of the ceremony still to go, and we stay until the finish, taking part in the dancing and all the rest. But the part that Doerniche played with the God of Discord was the heart of the festival, the center of our mystery.

It is painful for me to look backward. My past is accessible but no more compelling to me than any other record. It seems to have no bearing on me. It might have been about a different person entirely.

I am whoever I am now.

But this is not really satisfactory either. I maintain this record, even though I find it often incomprehensible upon rereading, because I seem to need a sense of continuity with my past.

It is easier for me to write it than to reread it. For sometimes these notes seem the work of someone I do not know at all. I cannot find therein the stylistic progression of a single personality.

Many of the things that I have noted down must have been fantasies or dreams. I can find no other way of explaining them.

I would like to know how Lanea became my wife. But perhaps it is better for me not to know.

Now it is another day, and I am in a different mood. I do not know why I harbor such sickly misgivings about the past. As Wolfing has pointed out to me, the past is always a state of potentiality, and its various outcomes can be known by one's state-of-being in the present.

Wolfing and the others are better friends than I deserve. They are rarely irritated with me, even when my alien education leads me into all kinds of inadvertent gaucheries. They view my behavior with the generous eyes of love, as I do theirs.

This is most particularly a special day for me—what they call here "a starburst day." It began very quietly and with no hint of what was to come. I was drinking my morning coffee and reading a book of poetry—S'thenm's experiments in the antique verse form called Helian. I must be the only person on Kaldor who has not read this miniature masterpiece. But at least I have the pleasure of reading it now and savoring the intricate and archaic web of words.

There was a knock at the door. Wolfing had come to call.

We spoke for a time of inconsequentialities. An outsider might have thought it a normal conversation. But Wolfing and I are friendship-bonded. This means that I cannot avoid reading the emotionality behind his facial expressions, gestures, and bodily movements.

So, although he did not say a word about it, I could tell that he was upset this morning.

One does not allude to what has not been verbalized, of course. Instead, I tried to think of a way of relieving my friend of pain while sparing him embarrassment.

My efforts were clumsy. But Wolfing noted my concern (as my group-friend he couldn't very well be unaware of it) and sought a means of putting me at my ease. But neither of us was particularly successful in our efforts. My grasp of the language has improved immeasurably since those naïve early days when I thought that words meant what they said and nothing more; but I still often falter when it comes to innate subtleties, which resemble telepathy more than a spoken language.

Wolfing was kind enough and brave enough to help me out

of my dilemma. I do not know what it cost him in self-esteem, but at last he managed to say, "I have been in a state of considerable tension these last days."

"How many days?" I asked.

"Three."

Therefore his tension dated from the festival of Sarameish. His face now was suffused with blood and he was biting his lip. The strain of having to give so direct a clue as that was telling on him. He looked as if he wanted to run out the door.

I was not in much better shape. The clue might have been enough for any Kaldorian; but would it serve a thick-witted Earthman?

I forced myself to be calm. The requirements of friendship were on me now, a heavy responsibility. I had to proceed by indirection and with utmost tact.

"It was a most successful ceremony," I said.

"That much is certain," Wolfing replied, his voice firm.

"I thought that Doerniche was splendid in his contest with Discord."

"I thought so myself."

"And Grandinang—what a superlative clown he made!"

"Our friend outdid himself," said Wolfing.

I was watching and listening avidly as he replied to me. Nothing I had mentioned so far had evoked in him a response congruent to his present state of mind.

"I suppose you had to sit among strangers?" I went on.

"Yes, that was my luck in the draw. But it did not matter. I was in excellent atunement with those around me."

"That was fortunate. . . . Did you see Eliaming? Our poor friend was seated nearly behind a pillar which partially blocked his view and must have impeded his catharsis. I consider that sort of thing a public disgrace."

"It's not as bad as all that," Wolfing said. "I talked to Eliaming afterward. He told me that his impaired visibility simply made him concentrate harder on the ceremony, with beneficial results."

"I am glad to hear that," I said. "I was worried, as was Lanea."

"Was she indeed?" Wolfing asked. "She shouldn't worry herself about such matters."

"But that is her pleasure!" I told him. "After all, we are a friendship-group! Lanea also hoped that Doerniche had not cut his fingers badly, and she hoped that Grandinang had not overexerted himself in his clown antics, and—"

"Yes, go on," Wolfing said.

"And most particularly she worried about you."

"Did she? Are you sure about that?"

"Of course!"

"She has not spoken to me since Sarameish," Wolfing said, and how he could not completely hide the wound in his voice!

I was on surer ground now, and I was able to speak with more of a show of confidence. "That very fact shows her concern! You know the proverbial reticence of women and how quick they are to conceal what they feel most. Lanea's love for you—"

"Love? Did you say love? That must be a considerable exaggeration, though a kind one."

I was sure of my ground now and in full stride across it. "I would not overstate a matter like that," I told him.

"Love! I can scarcely believe it!"

"Then you are the only man in Morei who does not know. Come, pull yourself together! Love is that natural and expected relationship whose beginning is always in the friendship-group. Surely you know that?"

"I do," Wolfing said hesitantly. "I know it in the abstract, at least. But one can never be certain of a particular individual beforehand. And frankly, I was afraid that you . . ."

I laughed. "You saw me as Captain Smashing, the jealous, possessive barbarian of popular comedy! Or as some twist-brained alien from an evil planet—which perhaps I am! But I'm not quite that bad, my friend! The gentle obligations of the friendship-group are as sacred to me as to you!"

Wolfing tried to protest that he had never had such thoughts and to reassure me as to the depth and fervor of his friendship. But I cut him off, accepting his emotion in advance. I was in a state of exhilaration, because for once I had directly intuited the situation and its requirements without having it spelled out for me. And that meant that I was beginning to realize my ambition of becoming like my adopted group and race, of merging with them and becoming indistinguishable from them.

"Wolfing," I said, "love is the most rarefied of the emotions; yet it must be taken palpably. Lanea is in the bedroom awaiting you. Take your love to her love, and take my love with you both!"

The last speech loses something in the translation, but it was stylistically suitable to the occasion. And Lanea had mentioned Wolfing once or twice over the past days, in neutral tones that might well have concealed love.

I fervently hoped that this was so. Wolfing was such an exceptional man and so handsome besides. And Lanea—how marvelous it would be for her, for all of us, if only she loved him.

Wolfing gripped my shoulder hard. Beyond words, we exchanged *d'bnai*, that inexpressible sharing of total agreement that goes beyond the limits of language.

He went into her bedroom and closed the door. I heard their muffled conversation, then silence, then a soft murmuring in which I could not distinguish one voice from another.

That seemed a good moment to leave the house. Outside, it was a glorious spring day. I walked through nearby woodlands in a state of incoherent joy. When I returned home some hours later, Lanea and Wolfing greeted me at the door. They had prepared a mock pot roast for me, my favorite dish. I could have wept for pleasure.

Mariska is plump and healthy and a little silly, much like her husband, Grandinang. Her skin is brown and tastes faintly of salt. She seems always to be in good spirits, also like Grandinang. She is like him in many other ways, too. Sometimes when I make love to her I can almost think that it is Grandinang beneath me.

Her apartment is always in a mess, her clothes don't fit properly, and I think that she doesn't wash enough. For me, this simply gives her added appeal. I suppose that it is the contrast to Lanea, who is fastidious as a cat. (An Earth cat.) I have been with Mariska continuously for two days and nights. We make love often, though not as often as people on Earth do in books. And we eat a great deal, usually in bed, and prop ourselves up with pillows and watch shadow plays on the Kaldorian equivalent of television: complicated dramas about ancient kings and queens and courtiers who spend most of their time debating various points of conduct. If Salvador Dali had gone completely crazy and rewritten Lope de Vega, the result might have been comparable. I can't figure out what the dramas are about—even the simple "Monsters of Contention" series involves assumptions that are quite beyond me. But it is pleasant to lie back against the pillows, sated and stuffed, and watch the intricate interplay of the shadows.

I stay in touch with Lanea, of course. We speak on the telephone every few hours. Wolfing had to attend to family business after a mere night with her, which left them both quite distraught. I suggested that she try Doerniche, who I judged more suitable to her present mood than Eliaming or Grandinang. But there I was guilty of a *faux pas:* Doerniche, having symbolically conquered the God of Discord, is now invested with the God's qualities. He is *goernu*—ritually unclean would be the nearest equivalent. He must abstain from all physical contact for a month, thus doing expiation for us all. At the end of that time, a simple ceremony will divest him of Godhood and *goernu.*

Surely I couldn't be expected to know all of this. But Lanea became angry at me, since I had spoken aloud of something she could not have. And in retaliation she put my red statuette into the closet and told Grandinang what she had done, and they had quite a cruel little laugh over it. This, in turn, might have provoked me into doing something really rash, and there might have been bad feelings for several days, even a week. But Mariska was there, thank God, and she put the situation straight very quickly.

Now that I think about it, it was all very much like a shadowplay, even to the solution.

Anyhow, Lanea and I had our first quarrel. From start to finish it lasted almost an hour, and it shook us both up considerably. I think it helped us to understand the depth and power of our love, however, and that is good.

Mariska and I are having such a marvelous time that I could almost envy Grandinang. Luckily, I am not forced to: since Mariska and I are in love, we are allowed by usage thirty days of unlimited access to each other. The only problem that this presents me with is Lanea, whom I love most dearly.

I must stop here and clarify my use of the word "love." There is no such word on Kaldor. On this planet, love is never expressed as a single (and therefore essentially simple) state of mind. Here love is recognized for what it is—the most complicated and exquisite of the emotions. There are about two hundred words in Kaldorian, all meaning love, each descriptive of a specific emotional state. Here they attempt to describe the infinite variety, the varying intensity, and the exquisite complications of that range of emotions which we on Earth lump together under the word "love."

No one here would use so vague a word as "love." The emotion I feel for Mariska is termed *mardradi* and refers to an uncomplicated, essentially physical attachment with two or more nonsexual sharings, the whole thing exerting a specified amount of psychic force. Whereas for Lanea, I am in *ourmge*, which refers to a profounder set of psycho-emotional states, both complex and exciting-complex, the semi-forbidden and therefore exciting taste for estrangement.

I suppose that love is as complicated on Earth as it is on Kaldor. But here neither its practice nor its mention are taboo. Quite the contrary. Here one can play with that infinitely rich instrument that love is.

In a sense, one must play. If Kaldor means anything, it means love.

I can't imagine why I stayed so long in that ridiculous Cape Cod cottage outside of Morei. I stayed of my own accord, so presumably I must have wanted it that way. It is so clear to me now that nobody lives outside the city except farmers, and nothing happens outside the city that makes any real difference.

Lanea and I have been lucky enough to find an apartment in Churtii Square, one of the really good districts, and in an area of third-greatest population density. It is a fantastic apartment, large, light and airy, beautifully furnished. I would have to be rich to afford such an apartment on Earth. Here I simply have to be from Earth: The apartment and other things were given to me by the Council. They have declared me a Living Art Object—on the basis of my uniqueness, of course, certainly not my beauty. All I have to do is whatever I want to do; for whatever the Art Object does is Art.

I haven't had much chance to actually live in my new home, however. Last week was particularly chaotic. A day and night with Blesse, Wolfing's wife, then two days and nights with

Mariska, whose feeling for me has moved into a higher category —somewhat to my discomfiture. Then home, but Lanea was with Eliaming due to a fault in the flow chart. Fortuitously, Hystoman came over one night early. She is Eliaming's wife, a tiny, dark, alert woman of great vivacity. This saved time but produced complications. We had to take our chart down to our flow-lawyer, lose an hour in his waiting room, and then sit around and twiddle our thumbs while he figured out the optimum sequences for the next week. And then, after Hystoman and I were at her home and just starting to relax, I remembered that we hadn't figured in Mariska's new category, which changes the temporality of the sequences and sometimes the sequences themselves. So Hystoman and I had to return to the flow-lawyer, and what with one thing and another we lost almost all of the day we had been trying to save. Luckily, Hystoman is a good sport and we were able to laugh about it.

But the end of complications isn't yet in sight. In four days Doerniche will be ritually cleansed and he and his wife Sara will rejoin our friendship-group. We all want them back, of course, but sometimes the sheer brute work of scheduling gets you down, even with expert help.

I think there is a way out of this, however. I have applied for a new apartment. We will soon see how highly they think of their Living Art Object.

The new apartment is really a fantasy beyond my wildest dreams. Fourteen rooms! Can you imagine that, fourteen rooms in the heart of a major city! And we are still on Churtii Square, which we had grown to like so much.

My question is answered. They think pretty highly of their Art Object around here.

This apartment is really the answer to our dreams. With all of us living here together—me, Grandinang, Wolfing, Eliaming, Doerniche, and our wives—we are able to do without clumsy flow-diagrams. We have changed our sexual practice to *beriang* —what might be termed "orgy" on Earth.

It is not an orgy, however, not in the sense that the word is used on Earth. Here, quite frankly, *beriang* is not much more than a convenient way of doing what we are already doing. It saves the tedious shuffling back and forth between rooms and spares one the attendant embarrassment of absent-mindedly going to the wrong bedroom on the wrong night. The purpose of *beriang* is supra-sexual. It is a state of heightened sensuality when all of us sleep together in the same room. (We had the apartment remodeled to permit this). Questions of precedence are lost when warm bodies touch and mingle. Intercourse (though of utmost importance to us all) becomes secondary to the joy of all of us sleeping together in each other's arms.

Beriang is practiced more or less continually by about a third of the population, I am told. I must admit that it has its drawbacks, albeit minor ones. The cumulative sexual force generated by ten bodies making love together night after night is apt to cause dizziness and hardness of hearing in some people. Then, too, some individuals cannot bear to be together for so long a time. These people, with their lust for solitude, are considered alienated and are the objects of special pity. And finally there are the minor irritations, the tossing and turning, moaning, groaning, snoring, all of which interfere with sleep. (One of the biggest public health projects in Kaldor is the search for a universal cure for snoring.)

One can always take advantage of the various empty bedrooms, of course, and upon occasion I have. But I don't like to leave my friends; it is a little rude and uncaring, and a native Kaldorian feels that much more strongly than I do.

Taken all in all, *Beriang* is a pleasurable activity and well worth accepting a few minor discomforts for. *Beriang* is the social state to which Kaldor officially aspires, for it exemplifies the utmost pinnacle in togetherness.

Despite this, Lanea and I have taken to sneaking off by ourselves to the upstairs storeroom, of all places! There I have put a mattress on the floor and Lanea and I make love there.

I do not know why we wish to be alone and away from all we hold dear. There is a little game that Lanea and I play with our toes. It is nothing to be ashamed of, but we have never done it in front of the others. Perhaps our desire to be alone comes down to that simple explanation.

Eliaming and I have had our brief fling and now it is over. We care for each other still, and our friendship is unimpaired, but we no longer experience that urgent desire that informed our relationship and made it magical. I still consider him beautiful, but I am no longer driven to possess him.

Lanea and I are back together again. For three weeks we were in *nacoteth,* which I can loosely define as a separation of brief duration, without loss of *ourmge,* the purpose of which is to increase one's sensory range and understanding *(hetti)* and to use that to achieve a more complex and fulfilling love status with one's partner.

Lanea and I came to a very satisfactory *hetti,* and our feelings for each other have now moved into the *chaardi* class, which is a deepening and spiritualizing of what we felt for each other in *oermge.*

We receive many compliments on this, as you can imagine. Fewer than 10 percent of the population achieve *chaardi,* and those who do become culture heroes. But, delightful as it is to excel, we have decided not to attempt further heightening of our relationship. One runs the risk in this, as in every skilled pursuit, of overspecialization, with attendant loss of contact with other vital currents of life. I think it is possible to overdo anything and that love on any higher level is auto-eroticism.

Lanea has become a little irritated with me since I formed a *doroman* (complex male sexual group) with Eliaming, Grandinang and Doerniche. (Wolfing regretfully declined our invitation. He is spending a few days alone in the hospital, recuperating from overstrained nerves. The poor man found himself in multiple reciprocal *ourmge* last week with Hystoman, Sara, and Merieth—a member of a cognate friendship-group.) This afforded the rest of us considerable amusement, since it is one of the standard farcical situations of the local equivalent of the Commedia dell'Arte. But it was not amusing for my poor ardent Wolfing. Still, he will recover in time for the Feast of Passage.

Lanea's annoyance at my *doroman* grouping is quite explicable. She herself has been afflicted with hysterical frigidity. She tried various combinations, both male and male-female. Her doctor prescribed strangers, but this also gave no relief.

It is not the first time that she has been taken with hysterical frigidity, and it is by no means an uncommon affliction on Kaldor. There are countless theories and a bewildering array of remedies. But most experts agree (as they often do on Earth) that time is the best cure.

Our state of love has altered, of course; how could it not? Now we are in *riothis*—asexual caring—and poor Lanea is ashamed to face her friends.

I am unable to feel much sympathy for her, though I would like to. When one is in one of the higher states of desire, it becomes almost impossible to achieve empathy with someone in a lower state. I do not wish to be callous; but I do have my *doroman*, which presently occupies my feelings.

I suppose *doroman* would be called a homosexual practice on Earth and would be scorned by the great preponderance of heterosexuals. But here no judgmental distinction is made. The race has a heterosexual bias (as biologically it must), but that has never become a behavioral mandate.

I wish I could describe the quality of *doroman*, for it is unlike anything else. But it is also like everything else, since it does not carry the weight of centuries of societal disapproval.

Sometimes I still wonder how I, an Earthman, could adapt so easily to these various practices. I suppose it is because it is all so normal here, and one tends to accept the standards of the society one lives with.

Whatever the reason, it is all good fun. I shall regret the ritual proscription of all sexuality except the religious variety which characterizes the Feast of Passage.

This is easy country to cross—gently rolling hills, short grass, scattered trees. Even the sun is good to us, shining with moderation and never allowing the nights to get too cold. Doerniche tells me that the character of the land will soon change for the worse, and the life-giving sun of this region will give way to a fiercer deity.

But we grow stronger as we continue our march. My feet are calloused now, and my shoulders have grown accustomed to the pack.

I continue to write this record, not out of desire but out of compulsion. It feels so futile: I can't remember any of the important things that should be noted. The Feast of Passage, for example, which I thought so memorable at the time. Now it is gone from my memory except for disconnected flashes that are more disturbing than enlightening.

I have asked the others for assistance in reconstructing that event. But they laugh at me rudely and tell me that only practical things are worth remembering.

At first they did not like to see me writing this journal. They feared that I was interfering with supernatural forces. Grandinang especially was upset. Once he tried to burn this journal—halfheartedly, though, as he does everything. But Doerniche saved the day by declaring that I was obviously the God-struck scribe of the group, that I was writing a heroic account of our journey, and that this account would be sung aloud at the In-gathering and bring all of us prestige.

I do not know whether he believed it or not. But it brought about a change of attitude. Now they urge me to write, and they make sure I hear of their puny daily exploits.

I have only a few disconnected fragments of memory concerning the Festival; but I am haunted by the feeling that something important happened at that time. My feeling is that something bad happened at that time. Or perhaps I don't mean bad, perhaps I mean monstrous.

We all took some drug, I remember that much. It was part of the Festival, had been so from time immemorial. I think it was a root that we washed, sliced and chewed, and we had special silk bags in which to spit the tough strands. We laughed a good deal about the ridiculousness of taking a drug. But Eliaming became serious and said that the drug was not necessary to the Festival; it was used simply to ease the participants and spare them anxiety. And he explained that the drug's effects were confined to about forty hours and that mild hallucinations had been known to occur at the peak of the drug's action but that the experience was controllable, and disorientation rarely occurred.

Eliaming usually made it his business to find out things like that. And he had also discussed with a doctor the advisability of me, an alien, taking the drug. The doctor told him that since I had no apparent difficulty with any of the other foods of Kaldor, I presumably would not with this one. But if I had any anxiety, he added, I should desist.

I had no anxiety. I took the drug with the others.

Then there is a gap in my memory. The next thing I remember is being in a place with many bright colors flashing. The colors were making my head hurt, the reds especially. After a while they began to take shape. They coalesced first into clouds, then into pillars, and finally into naked, faceless human shapes. Their scorching colors continued to burn my eyes until I, in self-defense, also began to pulse and glow with color.

That, I suppose, was a hallucination.

Next there was darkness and a man's voice—Doerniche's, I think (although he denies it), saying to me, "Of course, you couldn't have known, and of course, we couldn't have told you."

"But you're telling me now," I said.

"No, not really; I am merely substantiating what your being has just learned by becoming."

"I should have been able to guess it earlier," I said bitterly. "The evidence was there, if I had only looked."

"It would not have helped you."

"I know that," I said, and now I was weeping. "But I still wish I had known."

That entire conversation, which seems to have taken place in limbo, remains word for word in my memory. But I haven't the slightest idea what it was I should have known. Doerniche insists that the conversation never took place, and the others avoid speaking of the Festival or of anything except their present life and its difficulties.

I remember a crowd of people screaming, running in blind panic through the streets of Morei. Some of the old ones and the smaller children couldn't keep pace. They fell and were trampled by the others. And when the crowd had finally passed, they were unrecognizable as people.

I felt panic too (although I can't remember why) and raw terror. I saw that the crowd was dangerous, and I pulled myself up to a window ledge. I waited until they had passed, thinking them more of an immediate risk than anything else. But I paid a price for my independence. When I was ready to go the terror struck me most sharply. I thought it was after me alone, and I thought I would die from fright. I ran with the unthinking

exertion of a madman, and when I reached my group I thought
my heart would give out.

Earlier I remember being in a room. The walls were stone,
and they were covered with inscriptions that I couldn't read.
An oil lamp flickered in one corner.

Then I looked up and saw standing before me a naked man
with the head of a fox. In one hand he held a flint knife, in the
other hand a pine cone. The fox-head was a mask, of course. It
had to be a mask.

He said to me, "Now you know."

"What do I know?" I asked him.

"You know the face of the future."

I hesitated for a long time. Then I asked, "What are you?"

He replied, "A mirror."

I reached out to touch him, and my hand struck a smooth
surface. I put my hand to my face, and my fingers touched a
long hairy snout.

I think I screamed then. But I can't remember anything past
that.

There are a few more fragments which I can't put into any
particular order. They are not scenes; only a face, a landscape,
and a few disconnected sentences.

The face was a man's face framed in shaggy hair. He was
smiling, and his face was smeared with blood.

The landscape was desolate rocks almost hidden in mists on
a mountaintop. There was a pile of gray ashes on one side. The
mists parted momentarily and I saw innumerable pinpoints of
light far below me on the valley floor. Then the mists closed in
again.

There was a woman's voice saying, "All of our fine dreams,
and now we have come to this!"

And then another woman said, "This, too, is part of the
dream!"

And that is all.

I have been unable to make sense out of all this. I need time
to sort out hallucination from reality. But each day we trek,
and late in the afternoon we make camp and do all of the
things necessary to sustain life. And when that is finished I

write in my journal, and then I sleep.

I am always in a state of fatigue these days. I cannot think straight. I know that events have taken a very strange turn—several strange turns. But I am too tired to respond to them. I will sort them out when we reach the middle ground, which Doerniche says is only a few days' march from here.

There will be plenty of food and plenty of sleep at the middle ground. If we stay there long enough, perhaps I will dare reread the earlier parts of my journal and try to reconcile the contradictions which have become the substance of my life.

Our supply of food has been inadequate for some time. Most edible plants seem to grow in the lowlands. We are several thousand feet above sea level, I would estimate, and still climbing. Vegetation of any kind is growing scarce. We use up a lot of energy on the trek, and we are not replacing it.

We are undergoing changes in behavior. All of us have become prone to irritation, depression, sudden inexplicable rages. I do not know if our situation can account for all of this. I think we have undergone changes in personality dating from the Festival. We simply are not who we had been.

Good luck this evening! Just at dusk Wolfing spotted a deer. We all threw rocks at it, and through great fortune we broke its right foreleg and then pounded it to death with sticks. We built a fire, barely able to contain ourselves, for we had not realized how starved we were. We roasted the meat over an open fire, though this is a wasteful method, and devoured it half raw.

I had not expected to come across a city at this altitude. Nevertheless, we have come to the outskirts of one. We have lain for hours on a high outcropping, watching. There has been no stir of human movement, no vehicles on the streets, nothing at all. Or almost nothing. Wolfing says he can see packs of rats in the streets. All of us can see flocks of crows and the occasional buzzard searching the housetops for food.

We have had serious arguments over this city. Grandinang and all of the women want to loot the place; for cities always have storehouses of prepared food, to say nothing of gold and jewels. I would like to go into the place also, out of curiosity. But

Doerniche and Wolfing are in agreement for once opposing this. Doerniche argues that all cities are accursed and that we will take nothing but disease. Wolfing says that we couldn't carry much now and that we will come back and loot this place anyhow after the In-gathering.

It doesn't really matter who has the best of the argument. With Doerniche and Wolfing in agreement, the rest of us will do as they say.

Four sleeps later. We wish that we had looted the city when we had the chance, for now the country we pass through is truly barren. We are very high up now. We are beyond the tree line and still climbing. There are shrubs here but very few animals of any description.

Lanea no longer speaks to me, and she sleeps apart. She scorns me because I am a scribe and because her desire is to be mate to a warrior. She watches Doerniche constantly, and her eyes tell everything. Doerniche pretends not to see, for that would be beneath his dignity as clan leader. But the others see, and they laugh at me. I don't know what to do about this.

Why deny it any longer? We all detest each other. But it is family hatred that we share, not comparable to the hatred we have for other clans. It makes no sense at all when you consider how we had been before the Festival. But perhaps it should be viewed the other way: Our life before makes no sense in terms of our present condition.

Something truly miraculous. We were reaching the end of our strength, and Doerniche called a halt and prepared a fire. Eliaming began to chant to the ancestors and we all clapped in time. The holy light was in Eliaming's eyes, and he danced around the fire with a strength and grace that went beyond anything physical we had ever witnessed.

We are very lucky. Doerniche tells us that not all clans have a natural priest among them.

Eliaming's song went on and on and we danced to it, feeling no fatigue. Sometime before dawn the strength of the god touched Sara and she fell to the ground and tried to bite her tongue, but we put a stick in her mouth. And still we danced, for our faith was strong.

Then the god relented and sent us a bear. At first we thought it was a ghost because bears have no business so high in the mountains. But Eliaming knew it for what it was, and he directed us to kill it.

That was no easy task! The god permitted us to trap the bear in a little gully; it had to be the work of the god, for bears do not permit themselves to be trapped so easily. We showered the bear with stones, but this had no effect, and our courage began to grow larger than our hunger.

We looked to our strong men, Doerniche and Wolfing, and they looked at each other. There has been bad blood between them, for they both have the blood of leaders, although only one can lead here. But now they composed their differences for the good of the clan and because god was watching to see what we did with his favor. They took their spears and went forward.

The rest of us continued to throw stones to distract the bear. The spearmen went to the other side. (We didn't really have spears, only long shafts of wood with fire-hardened points.) The bear rose up on his hind legs and his little eyes flashed red. His head swung to and fro, and then he swung around and attacked Doerniche.

Then things happened fast. Eliaming let loose the god-scream, and that froze the bear in his tracks. Doerniche wedged the spear against a rock. Wolfing, who some of us expected to turn traitor at that moment, attacked the bear from the side, driving his spear deep just below the ribs.

The bear lunged at Doerniche but without his full impetus, which had been interrupted by the god-scream. Doerniche stayed cool and positioned his spear, taking the bear in the center of the throat. And then Doerniche rolled quickly out of the way of the slashing claws, suffering no more than a deep scratch from his shoulder to his hip. And even that was good, for the scar will win him much prestige.

Then the passion went out of us, and we stood silently and watched the bear kick and twitch and bleed to death.

Eliaming collapsed. He had paid a fearful price for saving us, and that will not be forgotten.

We feasted that night and drew strength from bear meat and bear fat. We sang the old songs that have been handed down from the dawn of time, led by Mariska, whose voice is as clear as running water. And then they all called upon me to tell them of the slaying of the bear, because that is the custom.

I made a show of reluctance, not entirely feigned, for my role sat uneasily upon me. But at last I stood up, and Grandinang put a rag around my head as substitute for the poet's chaplet. I stood in front of the fire and declaimed to them of what they had done, making their brave exploits even more heroic, for that is the way of retelling. After a while I was able to overcome my self-consciousness and act out the parts with my body. I did not think highly of my performance, but the others were satisfied. And Doerniche himself told me that I had done well, and that was an intoxicating moment.

That night Lanea slept with me, the first time in many nights. And afterward she put my head in her lap, traced the lines of my face with her fingers, combed my hair, and said that she would always love me.

It was a time to dream on. But in the morning we resumed our trek, laden down with bear meat, and Lanea was cold and distant again and seemed to regret the affection she had shown me.

We have had to lose an entire day. Grandinang twisted his ankle, and we cannot carry him and the bear meat. Grandinang is such a fool! But he is a very good fool, he amuses us all, and that is necessary.

This day of rest is welcome to me, for my thoughts and memories press heavily in my head, and I need to know the causes of things.

I am an alien, a man who came here from a planet called Earth. That much is certain, that much I always know despite whatever else happens.

I came to this planet and isolated myself for a long time. Then I began to live the life of the others. It was a civilized life as we know it on Earth. It was a peaceful life, devoted to love and the arts.

There was talk of danger, but the danger never came. Or did it?

Everything changed, and I changed along with it. There was a Festival. And then I was with my clan, marching to some far destination, leading a brutal life that somehow seems as natural to me as the other lives I have lived here.

What is the explanation for all this? Why have we turned our backs on civilization?

I cannot find the answers yet. But it steadies me to know what has gone before. I think that I am the only one who remembers.

Perhaps that is why I am the scribe.

I cannot record all of the quarrels we have had. But I must speak of the most recent one between Lanea and me.

It was dusk, a quiet moment. Our bellies were full, and we were in good humor because of that. It was a good time, and I reached out to take Lanea's hand.

She pulled away from me abruptly. I have never seen her face so contorted with rage. (Later I realized that she had been watching Wolfing and Elesse make love, and that had enraged her with jealousy.)

She said, "I do not want you to touch me again."

"You are my mate," I said, my voice reasonable. "Of course I may touch you."

"No!" she said. "Never again! I will be your mate no longer."

"How have I failed you?"

The scorn in her voice was indescribable. "How? In countless ways! But mainly because you are a scribe, and I was born to be mate to a warrior!"

"I work at an honorable profession," I told her. "I am satisfied with it, and so are the others."

"But I am not satisfied," Lanea said. "I will not sleep with you again."

"The nights will get cold," I said.

"For you, not for me. I am going to be Wolfing's woman."

"He has a woman."

"Then he will have two."

I looked around. The others were listening, waiting to see how it would come out. Wolfing had a grin on his face. Elesse, his mate, shuddered but said nothing. (She is a frightened little thing, and Wolfing dominates her completely.)

I looked to Doerniche. He sat on a stone wearing the bear-skin, and his face was remote and unreadable. I asked him what he thought of this, and he said, "What passes between you and your woman is no concern of mine, unless I wanted her for myself, which I do not."

Wolfing said, "She's probably more trouble than she's worth. But I'll take her if she wants to come."

Lanea said to me, "You see how it is, my dear? Go on scribbling in your notebooks; it is all you are good for. Write about this, too. Perhaps it will keep you warm at night!"

She rose to go, holding her little bundle of possessions in one hand. I seized her ankle. She kicked me in the shoulder with her free foot, and everybody laughed.

I got to my feet and slapped her in the face as hard as I could. She reeled back, yelling with anger, and then picked up a spear and came at me.

I sidestepped and kicked her feet out from under her. She went down hard and I threw myself on top of her. I was dimly aware that everyone was laughing and cheering as I hit her in the face. But then her fingernails raked my cheek and I went blind with rage and beat her in the body and face, hitting so hard that I grunted with each blow. She still tried to fight me off, but I could not be stopped, my honor had been violated, and now I was striking heavily.

I do not know how long I hit her. After a while, I realized that she was offering no resistance, and her head was hanging limp. So I stopped hitting her and splashed water in her face. When her eyes could recognize me, I raped her.

Our relations have improved considerably since then. Perhaps Lanea does not love me, but she does take care not to anger me. She sleeps with me when I wish it, and she keeps her mouth shut.

I think she may need another beating or two before she understands who her mate really is. She knows I am thinking this, and she takes care to give me no excuse.

I don't know if I will ever again have her love. But love is not important. What counts is that I have her respect, and I have not lost face among the men.

Last night all of the clans assembled here on this tableland, and you could see campfires in all directions, to the farthest horizons. All of the clans of this region were drawn to this spot by instincts I know nothing of.

Last night Lanea clung to me inexplicably and wept and

would not be consoled. I knew that some special understanding was being called forth from me, but I did not have the knowledge.

I asked her what the matter was. She said, "It is the end for us, and I am mourning."

"But why?" I asked. "What has happened?"

"Nothing yet," she said, "but it will."

I kissed her and said, "Whatever happens, I will be with you."

"No," she said, "this time it is impossible, this time it is the end for us."

I thought she was being hysterical. I said, "Is it another change? I have lived through all of the changes on Kaldor, and I am prepared to live through this one also."

"You cannot do the impossible," she said. "You are not of our stock. You do not share our potentialities."

"True, but I've done pretty well at adapting to your life."

"You have done miraculously well. . . . I am so proud of you! But there are some things that you cannot do."

I smiled at her. I was easy and confident. "Don't be so sure of that. I think that now I am more Kaldorian than Terran."

She looked at me fondly, as if I were a child. "You have been lover and friend, and you have lived our life to the fullest. But now it is at an end."

"You're wrong," I said. "It is not finished."

"I know," Lanea said, "and you do not know. This is not a matter of will power, not even a matter of love. We are from different planets! The rhythms of our lives are different. What must be cannot be forestalled. Nor would I change my fate, or yours. It is appropriate for us to live each in accordance with his own nature. To resent that would be to rage against the very nature and meaning of life."

All of that made very little sense to me. I knew that a change was imminent, but I had lived through other Kaldorian changes.

Nevertheless, Lanea insisted that I make love to her for the last time and then kiss her and walk away.

I did as she asked. I thought that I could change her mind tomorrow.

All of my clan sought me out. They kissed me and said goodbye. They walked away, each person in his own direction. Then

I knew that whatever else happened, it meant the dissolution of my clan, the loss of my family.

Eliaming was the last to go. He was crying, and he said, "We all had great pleasure with each other, Goldstein, and you were our family as we were yours. But now the law of the universe has been invoked, that like must stay with like, and it is a bitter time for us to go away from you."

"For the sake of what we have been to each other," I said, "tell me what is going to happen."

"I cannot tell you," he said. "I do not know. It is a mystery."

"Then how do you know that it is the end for us?"

"Because I know," he said. "That is blood-knowledge. It has nothing to do with our heads."

"Are you going to die?" I asked. "Is that it?"

He shook his head. "There is no death on Kaldor. There is only change. Goodbye, Goldstein."

"Wait!" I cried. "Is there nothing else you can say to me?"

"I can tell you a story," he said. "Once there was a baby mouse who lost its family. It wandered alone over hills and down valleys, lonely and afraid, and it grew weaker and weaker, and at last lay under a tree, near to death. Some grasshoppers came by and felt sorry for the little mouse. They fed it and took care of it, exactly as they would a baby grasshopper of their own. And the baby mouse lived and learned the ways of the grasshoppers and finally came to think that he was a grasshopper. And they were all very happy together, and they lived as one big family. And the mouse swore that he would never leave his family. But then winter came and the grasshoppers died, and the mouse was left alone. It was no one's fault: Grasshoppers live only a single season, whereas mice live for several."

"But you said there is no death on Kaldor!"

"Not for us who were born here."

"But for me there is death?"

"I do not know. Perhaps there is death for you here, since you are not of this place. But I do not know. Your life and its changes are a mystery to me, a greater mystery than we are to you."

"Is something going to happen to me?" I asked him again.

"I do not know!" Eliaming said. "You see the trouble with words? Nothing can be explained that you do not already know. I tried to talk about this for your sake, because I love you. But

I have said too much, or not enough, and have only caused you anxiety. Keep the memory of our love! Goodbye, Goldstein!"

So Eliaming, the last of my clan, went away.

People are scattered all over the hills. They seem to be waiting for some great event. I stay and wait, too. What else can I do?

It is evening now, and I sit by the fire, the last of my clan. All of the thousands have gone to sleep already, and their fires are burning out. I alone bear witness, but I am tired, too.

I cannot stay awake. But in the morning I am going to take some kind of action.

Now I am alone.

The thousands of people who covered these hillsides are gone. (This mere absence of something familiar is the most astounding sight I have seen in my travels.) They are gone, and they have left behind them only a litter: I am surrounded on these hilltops by burned-out fires, weapons, cooking pots, clothing.

All of their clothing is here. They left without their clothes. For me, this means that they vanished.

I cannot bring myself to accept what has happened. I suppose they left in the night. One of them may well have given me a drug. Then they all went away. Perhaps they left their clothes for some religious reason.

The alternative that I must accept is that they vanished.

I am in deep emotional trouble. I can feel that I am in trouble, and there is no one around here to help me. I am very lonely. There is company of sorts, because all of the animals have returned. This for me is inexplicable. They have been gone since late winter. But now they are back in a fantastic profusion. Birds, beasts, everything that walks or crawls seems to be on these hills.

I have not written in this journal for a while. There is nothing to write. I live here alone. They abandoned me. I suppose they found me unworthy. God knows, that's a fair assessment.

I suppose that is why I was sent away from Earth. I was unworthy to live with humans. They saw me for what I was, and they put me into a spaceship and sent me away to another planet, where I would have another chance.

But I couldn't make it here. I fooled them for a while, but ultimately I couldn't make it. But they were too kind to send me away. So instead they went away themselves, to some other part of the planet, I suppose.

It is only a matter of time before the animals learn what I am. For now, I have them fooled, too, as I have fooled so many others. They are remarkably tame. I don't think they have ever been exposed to anyone. They are shy like all animals but friendly. They come up to me and lick my hand. They sleep near me. But I must not grow accustomed to that; they will go away, too.

The ones who stay longest around me are those of my totem, the owl and the deer. They are the kindest of the animals. In a way, the deer have adopted me. One or more of them always sleep near me. The owls light on my shoulders, the only birds around here to do so.

Grass is covering the weapons and clothing. Time is passing, it is passing.

All right, I suppose I can put it together somehow. What the hell is so terrible about saying it?

All the people turned into animals.

I didn't because I wasn't born here.

They underwent a metamorphosis—not their first.

From the time I came here, the strangeness was evident. Their social institutions changed with bewildering speed. Overnight the norms had shifted and entirely different standards were accepted.

They changed from a formal, evasive culture to a loving, communal culture, to a primitive, distrustful culture.

But the metamorphoses of their lives go deeper than that. They change again, a physical change, like that of a butterfly or frog. Their births are somehow connected to the life cycle of the planet. To all of its life cycles, I should say.

It is a planet of reincarnation.

There is no mysticism here. It is the simplest, most basic truth. Men are reborn as animals.

And what are the animals reborn as?

Here, I don't believe that the cycle of births has any value judgment attached. They do not admit the existence of karma. One birth as one thing is as good as any other birth; for all things living are worthy of being lived. And besides, everyone will in time be born as everything.

It is reincarnation without death. Here there is only birth and change.

Naturally enough, there was no way in which I could have joined that cycle.

It is late in the summer. The days are golden. We are getting more frequent rains.

I have returned to Morei. Many of the animals have returned with me. They don't seem to mind the place at all.

Of course, it isn't really theirs. It belongs to the next human births.

Anyhow, the animals are going away. Or, more probably, they are changing. For a new growing season has begun here, and plants are crowding out animals.

I have moved out of the city again. It is fall now, and I am happiest sleeping among the members of my totem, the pines.

I do not have much to write. Time is passing, and I am living. I am starting to feel steadier. I am beginning to come together.

It is winter.

The animals are all gone. The plants are dead. The only thing alive in this place is me.

There will be new births in the spring, I am sure of that. Perhaps my friends will be reborn then. But perhaps I will be dead. Because death is always one of my imminent and unique metamorphoses.

I am going to stay here until spring. This will necessitate some hard decisions: I will have to live off the bodies of my friends, animal and vegetable, or perish myself.

Perhaps it is an ultimate human selfishness, but I cannot permit myself to die, even at this price. So I eat what I must, and I try to remember that everything eats and is eaten and that someday I will provide sustenance for whatever can use me here.

I follow the custom. I will not eat those of my clan. I eat as sparingly as I can of anything that once contained life. I wait, I dream. Will they return to me?

I pray it will be a short winter.

She is always herself, and carries without pretence, under her crown or her wide-brimmed hats, the same snowy solitary face. The name given to her, the *Divine,* probably aimed to convey less a superlative state of beauty than the essence of her corporeal person, descended from a heaven where all things are formed and perfected in the clearest light. . . .

—Roland Barthes, "The Face of Garbo"

THE TWENTY-EIGHTH DAY

BY KATHRYN PAULSEN

Hear the truth about the time before our days were numbered:

In the beginning was nothing but the Moon, no woman to worship Her light.

No one knows why from Her light, the only light, She made the many others.

From Her round heart She cast away Her flesh, and the light left it though it remained as tender as She.

Out of it She brought forth lesser lights, harder in their youth than She. They lived in Her darkened flesh, and She fed them, and they sang to Her.

Those lights that remained still She called Her sons. Though they were part of Her, Her fire had cooled in them. They had lost Her power and could not bring forth others from themselves.

Those that danced the Moon called Her daughters. They were not only of Her flesh but of Her spirit, and out of their own dancing lights they brought forth other lights, both still and dancing.

Now the Moon had a son, called earth, whose light went out entirely. That he should yet be useful the Moon sent some of Her other children to fall upon Him. Feeding upon the dead earth, these stars weakened and began to forget their Mother.

From the earth the Moon's fallen children could watch a brother, the sun, who wanted to make of himself another, as his Mother and his sisters could. The more the sun traveled the greater was his discontent, and he spoke to his brothers on earth, saying:

Our sisters, who, like our Mother, can make children, know the secret of life. They keep it from us, and we will learn it only if we surround them and hold them and stop their dancing to make them tell us.

This they did. They captured their sisters and told them: We will not free you till you give us your secret.

But the sisters did not know the secret and could not tell. Ask our Mother, the Moon, they said. It is Her secret.

But the sun and his brothers said to each other: The Moon will never give us Her secret. We must take it from Her.

With the body of the earth they built a tower to climb to the Moon. But the labor of an entire day brought them no closer to Her. The higher this tower of dead earth rose, the farther the Moon withdrew.

Ah, She is fleeing us, Her sons said. We must build higher. We must force our sisters to bear more children to labor with us till the tower reaches Her.

Even when their tower collapsed the sons still thought they had frightened the Moon. They saw Her turn from them.

But She did not turn away from fear. She turned from sorrow for Her captive daughters and for their children who would soon forget the source of their light, and die.

And it was not till the twenty-eighth day that the Moon again looked upon earth, though some say it was the twenty-seventh day or the twenty-ninth.

Take off your rings
at the first gate. At the second,
your crown of lapis lazuli.
You must leave your golden
breastplate at the third, and below
the gallows where he hangs
who forgot you, and will not rise,
break your mother's scepter.

—Marilyn Hacker, "Sisterhood"

CALL ME ISHTAR

BY RHODA LERMAN

"Lady, we gotta put you under arrest."

"The charges, sirs?" Ishtar asked politely.

"Indecent exposure?" the policeman answered, shrugging his shoulders.

Ishtar watched the flight of a pigeon above her head and walked, following the arresting officer, toward a patrol car. It would be unfitting, she felt, if this were indeed a final scene, to walk in humiliation or even in humility, which was hardly her style, whining that her father had forsaken her. As others had done. They had cried for their fathers because they knew full well it was their mother leading them to their ends, usually irrevocably and with justification. The men at the golden oak booking desk asked Ishtar if she wished to call her lawyer and her husband.

"They are the same."

"Is your husband a lawyer?"

"In the strictest sense."

"Don't book her yet. Wait until he shows," the arresting officer advised a clerk who seemed to be fascinated by Ishtar's hem. The police were exceedingly embarrassed. She had wished them to be impressed.

"I'll stay. Really. Please write my name, Ishtar, Queen of Heaven, in the book. The charges, bail and all that. As I have seen it on television."

She had hoped also for something if not dramatic at least melodramatic, something cruel and heartless that would make for good text and legend when the police records would be demanded by the populace and would be iconized in small golden houses to be carried into whatever wilderness was left.

"No, we'll wait for your husband. We'd rather he took the responsibility."

Ishtar grew powerfully angry and twisted the knob from a golden oak chair, until, unable to remain still, she stood on the chair and addressed the startled group, arms raised above her head to the large fan on the ceiling. "I, even I, Queen of Heaven, take the responsibility for the bursting of the factory, for the disorganization of your schools, for the death of a rabbi, hanging quite strangled in his cloakroom, for the organ at the Temple, which has burst its pipes and caused considerable damage, for the radical activities within your churches, for the ecstatic states of your children. All of it. Furthermore, my own husband, Robert, has grown impotent from fear of my power. That also, which I regret, I have done."

"Lady, is this a confession? Come down. Do you want this to be a confession?" The clerk lifted his pen.

Ishtar beat upon her chest. "I confess to no one. It is truth I speak." They shifted on their feet. "I am responsible. I would like a record made at what time I came in and at what time I went out. I want it on your blotter."

"You're not responsible for anything you say unless your lawyer is here," the arresting officer advised her, his teeth grinding behind his cheek meat. Something shorted in the electric overhead fans, which began to whine fearfully from their stations in the ceiling.

"I, even I, Queen of Heaven, am responsible. Utterly. You do not believe me." Angry amber tears coursed over her cheeks. "You do not believe me. Here, I will show you."

It was just as Robert pushed open the double doors, his rep tie sailing behind him in the wind and behind that a small friend-of-the-family judge, that Ishtar lifted her skirts and, howling, displayed her feathers. But the men had looked away at the doors and the clerk hid his face and she went unnoticed. She stomped her foot in the chair and aimed two golden acorn knobs through a windowpane. It shattered convincingly.

"Are you all right, baby?" Robert, his hands shaking to his shoulders, questioned her, and gently, albeit palsied, guided her to sit. She allowed him to guide her.

"I'm well. I have done all of these things. Do not call me baby."

The night before, when the starter broke on her small car, Ishtar had attempted to push it with Robert's many horsed station wagon and had shattered the rear end of the small car twice, while Robert, his face incredibly contorted in the rearview mirror, held the wheel of the small car. They had not succeeded in starting the small car, although Robert had succeeded in sitting quite still as she drove the large car into the small car many times. They argued on the road about Ishtar's incredible mechanical incompetence. He knew her as incapable. But she could see in his eyes, in the courthouse, above the neatly striped tie, the gray flecks of his supernatural rising toward the centers of his sharp black pupils. He blinked. Between his blinks she saw everything of his nightmares and visions that he remembered from high school *Macbeth* and he removed his glasses to cleanse the lenses on a navy blue handkerchief which was torn. Ishtar dismissed the touch of guilt she felt for the torn handkerchief. She was pleased, however, with the disintegration of his rationality.

"I'm a notary public." Robert turned to the judge, seated now before the golden oak desk. "If that helps."

"If you take her home in your custody, we won't have to take further action tonight."

"Robert, I wish them to write my name in the book. When I came in and when I went out."

"In the morning," the judge murmured. "Women, Robert, often want to take the responsibility for major events. They come in here and confess to every murder, fire, theft. Even suicides. I've had three women at once confessing to the same suicide. Your good wife wishes to confess to many things. Her charge is indecent exposure. She may have been suffering from a temporary instability. Come here, dear." The family friend judge addressed Ishtar.

"I chose to expose myself." Ishtar fought the petulancy in her voice. She was frightened that she would, in some grotesque turn of justice, be saved.

And denied.

She stood before the small judge, passing her hands over his head and withdrawing a sack full of ashes and three large acorns. "We'll get this straightened out. As soon as the excitement dies down." He leaned across his desk to pat her head. "I've known your husband since he was a boy." She sprayed Easy-Off into the eyes of the judge.

Ishtar spat the three acorns, one after the other, at his shining forehead and, squinting at him, laughed low, deeply and crookedly within herself. The judge gestured for a cloth for his eyes. To the arresting officer, Ishtar solemnly, as Robert led her out, awarded the screws from the fans, the large oak chair and a particularly manic grin. Claire stood outside with a zoom lens camera, photographing the event. Ishtar threw her a kiss and an acorn. Behind her the fans were blowing ashes into the courthouse, filling the rooms and covering the faces of the people. There would be no Youth for Christ this time to clean up after this exposure, which, although not indecent, was real.

. . . The raw material of music is found in the expressive noises and cries which human beings as well as animals give vent to under excitement of any kind; and their contagious power is shown, even in the incipient stage, by the sympathy which they evoke in other sentient beings.

—C. Hubert H. Parry,
The Evolution of the Art of Music

THE HARP THAT CONQUERED HELL

BY BEEBE THARP

Euterpe had come to the grove that afternoon to be by herself. She was downhearted—all the Muses were, except Calliope, who was desolate. In such cases as this an aunt's sorrow cannot be measured against a mother's anguish.

It was not as though her nephew were dead, Euterpe had to remind herself again. Indeed, her wretchedness might have been less if *he* had been Death's victim, for, alive, his sorrow infected them all, and each Muse, sharing his wild sorrow, weighed down her sisters' spirits in turn. Human beings died all the time, and it was always rather pathetic when they did, but really, this was out of all proportion!

She laid her slender hand upon the rough surface of a rock, remembering the time—how many years ago?—she'd seen this same rock dancing unrestrainedly, here in the grove of Zone, to the solemn measures of her nephew's harp.

Orpheus's harp! It had been Apollo's gift, and she herself had given the boy his first lessons on it. It was silent now, for he had wrapped it in the bridal veil of his beloved, lamented Eurydice, vowing nevermore to touch those magic strings till he too had descended to the dismal, subterranean halls of Tartarus!

Suddenly the stillness of this sylvan scene was broken by the sound of a child's laughter. Euterpe looked up, feeling an irresistible charm penetrate the chill of her heart. There he stood, not ten feet off, a boy of six or seven years, still chubby with baby fat. He was aiming a tiny bow and arrow at Euterpe, who waved his playful threat aside with a sad smile. "Not now," she said.

"You've been crying," the boy observed, replacing the arrow

in his little quiver. Even in so brief a phrase Euterpe was quick to note the musical qualities of his voice.

"Am I?" She brushed away a tear. "Perhaps I have a reason."

"On such a day as this!" the little archer exclaimed. "With these poplars bursting into leaf at the joyful prospect of another spring?"

"On such a day as this—alas, yes! For even as these same leaves were splitting from their buds, my nephew was married to a charming girl."

"If he had been your beau, that would be cause for weeping."

"Hear me out, naughty child! Within a little month, in the vale of Tempe, by Peneus's bank, Death had jealously ripped the young bride from her husband's arms. Now he mourns, and all who loved him mourn as well."

"Even Death," the child said, turning aside his face to conceal a mischievous smile, "must sometimes feel the pinch of desire. Surely you've heard the tale of how, pierced by the dart of love, he bore off Ceres' daughter, fair Persephone, to his dark kingdom. But tell me, what nymph or dryad has captured his heart this time? What young husband has he cheated of his pleasure?"

"Eurydice is dead," the Muse whispered, not so much in answer to the impertinent question as to unburden her heart of the pain that would, in moments, clench it again in its brutal grasp. "She is dead, and Orpheus, her husband, my sister's only son, is inconsolable."

"What! Orpheus? The son of the Thracian kind Oeagrus? Orpheus, who sailed to everlasting fame aboard the *Argos*?"

"Even he."

"It cannot be. Why, scarcely a week ago I heard him as he walked among the hills of Thracian Pieria. He sang the praises of Hymen, and even the birds stilled their flight that they might better harken to the raptures his fingers awoke in the seven-stringed harp."

"Oh, speak no more of his music! He has vowed never to touch those strings again."

Involuntarily Euterpe pressed her hands to her bosom. The boy's reckless chatter had reawakened a memory that gave a fresh edge to her sorrow. For handsome young Hymen had heard Orpheus's paeans, and in gratitude he had come to the wedding to give his blessing to the union of the rhapsodist and

his doomed bride. But when Hymen had raised his torch, its
fires unaccountably died. Euterpe's eyes had smarted from the
acrid smoke for hours afterward—a certain premonition of the
more bitter tears they soon must shed.

"Orpheus keep silent?" the boy scoffed, striving to reassure
himself. "Why, he could no more keep his fingers from the
strings of his lyre than I could stay mine from this bow."

"I could wish, for the sake of Art, that I shared your convic-
tion, little one. But he has made his vow."

"Never again to play? Never to sing?"

"Never," she affirmed. "Unless . . ."

"Unless . . . ?" He smiled coaxingly. "Yes?"

"Unless he finds himself in Death's halls, united with his love
again."

"In Tartarus?" The boy could not repress the shudder that
convulsed his pretty shoulders.

Euterpe bowed her head. "There."

No sooner had she turned away from the child than she heard
. . . But she could not believe her ears—had he giggled? Even
the gods of Olympus respected the power of Death. Who was
this child that he could hold Hell's power in such despite?

Her gray eyes glanced up, afire with stern reproach, but he
no longer stood where he had been. She looked around the
grove, where twilight now was weaving black bands of mourning into the branches of poplars that once had danced for joy
at the twanging of Orpheus's harp. The mysterious child had
vanished, and Euterpe was alone, once more, with her
thoughts.

Despite every argument his friend Coronus could adduce,
Orpheus steadfastly refused to leave the spot where the corpse
of his child-bride, his forever-dear Eurydice, had been discovered by the dryad Dyblia. It was a gloomy place, at the heart
of the vale of Tempe. The high cliffs, which towered up a thousand feet and more, cast the river Peneus and its banks into a
deep shade, giving them the aspect of one of the murky tribu-
taries of the Styx—Acheron, perhaps, the stream of woe, or
birdless Aornis.

Coronus posted two guards unobtrusively to watch over his
old friend and to prevent him, in the ecstasies of grief, from

doing irremediable harm to himself. Then Coronus returned to the high-walled city of Thessalian Gyrton, where he reigned. Orpheus heeded his friend's departure as little as he had his presence. Nothing existed for him but the pain of knowing his Eurydice was dead. Against Death, as against no other enemy, he was helpless.

Never when Eurydice had been alive had his passion so dominated his every thought as now, when she was lost to him forever. Eurydice dead—it was unthinkable! Yet it had come to pass. How? How? Again and again his thoughts returned to the moment when, after following the hysterical Dyblia along the twisting riverbank paths to this accursed spot, he'd discovered her slim young body, which always before had so pliantly yielded to his ardent embrace, stiff now with death. He had pressed the warmth of his lips to the coldness of hers. Oh, anguish beyond bearing! But the cruelest memory was of her eyes: eyes that stared yet did not see, eyes upon which, three days later, he'd seen his mother Calliope reverently place two copper oboli, which Charon would exact for his labors when he ferried the girl across the foul-smelling Styx. Orpheus had been ready then to smash his golden lyre, the gift of a god, against the glazed coffin in which her body had been sealed, shattering both with the same blow. Calliope had gently intervened, handing him his darling's wedding veil, which still bore upon it a trace of the marjoram that had scented her hair. It was then, wrapping the sheer cloth about his harp, that he'd vowed never more to lift his voice in life-enhancing song. Only a silence equal to theirs was fit to be dirge for the dead.

He pressed his face into the humid earth where she had lain, as though by the force of his desperation he might penetrate to the world beneath, where Eurydice was held eternally a prisoner, kept from sunlight, happiness, and love.

How long he remained prostrate in this manner he could not have said. He was roused by a pair of small hands tugging at his shoulder and by a voice that, though childish, was strangely stern in its reproach.

"What, Orpheus! Will you root up the ground like a swine? Come, show your grief some manlier way than this!"

The odd creature who addressed him so intrepidly was only a small boy, not taller than the midpoint of a grown man's thigh.

He had been playing at the hunt, for he wore a diminutive quiver on his back, which contained arrows and a bow scaled for his own slight strength.

Orpheus stilled his first angry impulse, for there was something about this overbearing child that had caused the keenest portion of his pain to abate.

The boy smiled. "Then you remember me?"

"Have we met before?" Orpheus asked.

"Only once, but recently. It was in Thrace, not long after your return from Colchis."

"I've spent long years in Thrace, and many children of that land have pranced to the tunes I've played for them."

"It was to hear you play again, Orpheus, that I came here, for your music thrills me more, almost, than the chase." He touched one of his tiny, bronze-tipped arrows in emphasis.

"If I took up my harp today, the sounds I'd make would not set you dancing."

The audacious child replied by clapping his chubby hands in gleeful self-applause. "Oh, nothing shall ever stop *me* from dancing!"

"Then leave me. Find a more sunny glade for your sport, unless you would dance on the grave of my bride Eurydice."

"What—Eurydice dead, and buried here!" The child feigned surprise (though he knew all these matters very well, since it was he who had spoken with Euterpe a short time before in the grove). "What man or god would dare perform such a deed?"

"Neither god nor man, but a viper, hidden beneath the white petals of a wood anemone. Her heel bore the imprint of its envenomed tongue when I found her, where you find me, cold upon the ground, as cold as I might wish to be myself, without her."

"Oh, cowardly to wish your own death when you might better wish your love alive again."

"If mere wishes could restore life . . ." Orpheus sighed.

"Then let your music achieve what wishing cannot."

"Beardless tempter, leave me now. You shall not trick me into breaking my vow. For I have sworn that until I've joined my own Eurydice in dark Tartarus I shall not touch lyre or phorminx, nor play the flute or syrinx, nor even, were I invited by Lord Apollo himself, open my lips in song."

"Then join your bride where she has gone, and charm Hades and his wife, as once you charmed the stones and trees of Zone —and me."

"Conquer Hell with a harp!" Orpheus's impatience with the child verged on anger. He would have gone away had not his grief fastened him to this plot of ground as securely as iron fetters.

"Are you afraid then?" the boy asked slyly. "There was a time, I've heard, when Orpheus dared pit his voice's skill against the Sirens' song."

"But this mad scheme of yours—it can't be done. No living man can cross the Styx."

"Then enter by the back door—through Thesprotian Aornum."

"Three-headed Cerberus guards that entrance."

"Rather say, Orpheus, that he has . . . six ears!"

Orpheus slapped his thigh. "I'll do it!"

"Make me a promise before you set off. I fear by the time you've returned you'll have forgotten the little boy who helped you."

Orpheus picked up the child and kissed him once on each rosy cheek. "Name your price. I'll pay anything."

"Only this—that once you are back in this brighter world I may hear you play your harp whenever I come by. You see, I dote on music, and there have never been songs to equal yours."

"You have my word—and now, if you know it, point me the way to Thesprotian Aornum!"

His journey had taken him westward, through wilder and wilder territory, until at last he stood at the door of the cave. A chill wind swept across Aornum's fetid waters and, as a flute player's breath stirs music from the emptiness of a reed, whistled in the fissure in the rocks, creating weird sounds.

With one backward glance at the louring sky, Orpheus entered the antechamber of Tartarus, his harp slung across his back so that his hands would be free to grope his way down the steep, rocky descent.

He continued for hours, moving ever deeper but without any sign that he had attained Tartarus itself. He had expected his eyes gradually to grow accustomed to the gloom, offering him a more trustworthy guide than his outstretched hands, but the blackness remained absolute. Though he'd brought a lamp and oil, he did not want to advertise his presence unnecessarily.

Then without warning he heard, bearing down on him from every direction at once, a pack of savage hounds. By the volume of the sound he judged there must be fifty of them, and he could not repress a fear that he would be torn to pieces before he could unstrap the harp from his back.

A body lunged past him, knocking him sideways to the stony floor. But at last the harp was free. As his fingers sounded the first ringing chords, the great bow of the lyre shimmered. By the time his song was through it glowed like the brightest constellation in the night sky, filling the whole cavern with an uncanny luminescence.

With the first notes the fierce baying had been stilled, and now by the light of his harp Orpheus could see that it had not been a pack of dogs but the single guardian of this place, Cerberus, whose three heads hung lolling now, spittle running from the corners of the open mouths, swaying gently in time to the music.

Inadvertently Cerberus's vigilance had done Orpheus a service, for he had been knocked over at the very edge of the river of Death. One step further and he would have been plunged headlong into the treacherous currents of the awful Styx! It had been a narrow escape.

Entering Hell via Thesprotian Aornum, it was possible to cross the water by means of widely spaced steppingstones, and this Orpheus began to do, while continuing his song. Orpheus had reached the middle of the Styx when he discerned the figure of Charon, rapidly approaching in his huge skiff. Orpheus had entered Tartarus by the long detour of Aornum precisely in order to avoid the dreadful ferryman. How ironic that his singing should have attracted him! Now, hurry as he might, he couldn't hope to reach the other side of Styx before the black, low-bottomed boat was upon him.

Charon lifted his mighty barge pole, as though to strike the harp from Orpheus's hands, but instead he only plunged it deep into the muck of Styx, so as to hold his boat steady against the current. As the harp's music had charmed savage Cerberus, so it charmed his master now. Charon's strong arms trembled with the effort of resisting the current, but he willingly endured the strain so that he might hear another measure of the song. His glittering eyes had misted over with the beginnings of emotions that he could not have named.

A daring idea entered Orpheus's head. Rather than cover the whole distance to Death's throne on foot he might step into Charon's ferry and travel the rest of the way in style and comfort. The old fellow seemed to have a taste for music, and Orpheus, now that he was not violating his oath by playing the harp outside Tartarus, found considerable relief in the exercise of his talent.

He stepped gingerly from the rock to the flat bottom of the skiff, careful to place his foot precisely in the middle so as not to overturn it. Despite this precaution, the boat rocked, and Orpheus, to keep his balance, stretched out his hand. For a second his song was suspended, but this was long enough for Cerberus to lift his heads, a low growl rumbling up from his single throat. Even Charon seemed affected by the brief interruption: his eyes narrowed and grew colder. Then the song was resumed, and with it a calmness settled back on the old man's spirit.

The boat moved onward into the darkness of Hell, Orpheus's lyre burning like a lamp at the bow, Orpheus's music filling the vast expanse of Death's kingdom from one end to the other.

Even the wild waters seemed to flow more easily, becoming slow and mild as they bore the singer toward his goal.

She wondered how long she had been dead. Here in the perpetual evening of Tartarus, it was impossible to keep track of the time. Day or night, May or April—such questions only mildly worried her. After the first shock, death was surprisingly undramatic. Things just didn't matter as much. It was that, the mildness of it, that distressed her most.

Here she sat, beneath the spinning wheel to which poor Ixion had been bound, amidst the worst torments that Hell could offer, and it was difficult to feel . . . anything. Horror? No; nor compassion. Why did she keep returning *here?* She was free to spend her time with the rest of the blessed in the fields of Asphodel, where the very mud was strewn with Death's worthless hoard of gold and precious stones. Yet she came here, among the torments of the damned.

A vagrant melody floated through her mind, a love song Orpheus had sung to her the first day they'd met. She pursed her lips and tried to whistle the refrain, but somehow after three or four notes she lost hold of the melody. His tunes always seemed so simple until you tried to repeat one of them yourself.

She remembered how, once, in Thrace, Orpheus had . . .

Ah, that was it—she *remembered!* How much sweeter, what a blessing it would be to *forget!* One sip from Lethe, a single drop licked off her fingertip, and she would be released from the agony of recalling all the pleasures that could no longer be hers. Then, numb and knowledgeless, she might wander Asphodel's fields with all the other bloodless ghosts, feeling the same vast indifference, except on the rare occasions when the earth above their heads dripped with the blood of sacrifices. Then, oh, how they would rush together, like pigs to a trough, to soak up the offering and, for a fleeting moment, to enjoy a borrowed life.

Eurydice, however, on arriving in Tartarus, had refrained from tasting the water of Lethe's cypress-shaded pool. Deliberately to abandon her memories of Orpheus, however painful they were to her, seemed an unimaginable betrayal. Instead she had resorted each day to the other pool, where a white poplar rustled its undying leaves—the pool of Memory.

Again the tune returned to her. This time it seemed she could feel the very air of the place trembling with the sound of the harp strings, but she knew this could not be. There was no music in Tartarus; the music was in her own grief-distracted mind.

The spinning wheel above her shuddered to a stop, and stoical Ixion gasped.

A profound and causeless agitation possessed Eurydice. She rose from where she had been sitting and began to hasten across the torture beds. Everywhere around her the punishments had been intermitted: Sisyphus was resting from his eternal labors; the vultures had stopped eating Tityrus's liver; Tantalus's eyes were closed in blissful indifference to the specters of ever-vanishing pleasures.

All of them seemed to hear the imaginary music.

Was she going mad? Was this why the other shades refrained

from drinking at the pool of Memory?

She ran faster, scarcely conscious of where the path was leading her, and it was as though he were after her again, the bearded stranger, his rough hands grabbing for her chlamys, his heavy footsteps pursuing her like an avalanche.

He'd seemed, at first, such a pleasant man, but then . . . What had he told her his name was? Aristaeus? Had Orpheus ever learned the reason she had vanished?

She stopped short, swallowing a cry of pain. Her foot had come down squarely on a sharp amethyst, just where the serpent had bitten it. Touching the tender spot, she remembered once more the terror of those moments alone on the dark banks of Peneus, trying to hold on to a breath of life until Orpheus would find her. A final kiss had not seemed too much to hope for, and then perhaps he might have filled her last moments with an illusion of timeless love by the enchantments of his art. Fate had not granted her even this small boon. Her body was cold before he'd come. She'd fallen into the sleep from which this—dark Tartarus—was the only awakening.

The Orphic music grew louder. In the fields of Asphodel, where she now found herself, the spirits were not milling aimlessly in their usual manner, but all moved with one impulse toward Death's throne, from which the magnificent music seemed to issue. It must be that somewhere in the world above priests were preparing a sacrifice of hecatombs on behalf of some war party anxious to appease Death. Yet the bearing of the shades seemed almost peaceful, without that restless yearning that would possess them before a blood sacrifice.

The music had become a tumult that mixed a maenad's delirious joy with a sadness no less extreme, and because it could not be real, because it was only a trick of Memory gone mad, it was a torment worse than any she had witnessed through all the length and breadth of Tartarus. Her memories had become a flock of crook-beaked birds feasting on the scraps of her rational mind.

To hear his music and yet be denied his presence, his love . . .

No, she would not endure it! She would *accept* forgetfulness.

The white cypress of Lethe stood close at hand. Though her heel pained her too greatly to allow her to run, she limped resolutely toward the waters she believed would deliver her from the unendurable sadness of this delusory music.

Stooping gracefully, she reached out toward the dark surface. The very waters of the pool seemed to tremble in sympathy with the unreal, cascading melodies, but no sooner had her hand touched the icy water than the music ceased.

She lifted a cupped hand to her mouth.

A hand caught hold her wrist. His hand. She turned to face him, not yet ready to believe that it was not an illusion.

It *was* Orpheus, himself, here in Tartarus. Alive. Breathing. Touching her.

They both watched the Lethean water trickle through her fingers. Then they were in each other's arms, and his warm lips were pressed against hers.

It seemed as though they'd waited all their lives for the happiness of this moment.

I have seen elsewhere ruined houses and stat-
ues both divine and human: it is always man we
are dealing with.

—Montaigne, "Of Vanity"

EXTINCTION
OF CONFIDENCE,
THE EXERCISE
OF HONESTY

BY MICHAEL CONNER

On a ridge at the quarry's edge, overlooking the marble (and the mud) of Acros, young Terues the sculptor and Paros the old quarryman sat watching waves of heat from the valley obscure the image of the city below them. They had sat there for a time without speaking, listening only to the sounds from the quarry: the overlapped poundings of the mallets that drove the olive-wood wedges into cracks in the marble and the occasional wrenching crack as the water-soaked wedges expanded and fractured a block away from the solid vertical face of stone. Paros had something on his mind, Terues knew, otherwise he would not have called him away from his work to come here. Finally the older man did speak, his voice gruff.

"Tell me, Ter. You think yourself honest, don't you?"

Terues stared at him as if he had been asked a question that needed no answer. Was the old man playing with him? "If I didn't, I would not be able to practice my art. In order to copy what I see in nature I must be honest."

Paros smiled. "You answer confidently. Your honesty! That's why you cover your birthmark with a cream, isn't it?"

"Why, that's something else entirely! It's not my fault that the people in Acros consider birthmarks unlucky, along with the oval shape, which is unlucky too. If I didn't cover it, I'd never be able to even approach the Guild with my work! *I'm* not ashamed of it; it's other people who fear it. . . ."

Paros shook his head, still laughing. "Don't get excited, Ter, I know, I know. Myself, I'd rather look down on Acros than walk around inside it. Anyway, you see that one cannot always be completely honest. But do not doubt that there will be a time when you will have to be. When that time comes, you'll have no use for the Guild. That's why I asked you to come today." Paros turned toward the pit and whistled so loudly that Terues closed his eyes. "Terues," he said, "do you know what fire-geode is?"

The young man had heard of the substance, though he doubted that it actually existed. "I've seen it, I think. Some of the women at Court claim their jewels are such. Though most of those baubles are cold glass and certainly no living crystal."

Paros became serious suddenly. "Last week we found a large piece along a fracture line. My men prevailed upon me to destroy it immediately, but I wished to give it to someone who could carve it."

"You have a piece of geode? How do you know?"

"It has the characteristics. When I was in Service in the jungle colonies, I saw many such pieces, some most impressively carved, all of them living. None so large as what we found here, though."

There was a series of lurching squeaks from behind them. Terues turned and saw a mule-drawn cart led by a short sullen-eyed man approach. On the cart, lashed with lengths of thick hempen rope, was an almost perfectly egg-shaped piece of brownish stone that wobbled strangely as the cart bounced over shards of rock along the path. The quarryman stopped the cart next to them. Terues stood up and touched the cold surface of the geode, imagining as he did so that he could feel some sort of heat-drawing vibration just beneath its surface. Ridiculous fancy! According to what he knew, the stone was a natural casing for the crystal inside. It was supposed to be most beautiful and rare, hence valuable.

"The men wanted you to destroy it? Why?"

"Why don't you ask Gerro here?"

"All right. You. Why do you fear this stone?"

The man regarded Terues with some contempt. "No matter what you believe," he said, "the stone lives! Inside there is a woman of light who struggles against her release from the stone. The crystal can project her fire if it is disturbed, revenge against those who take her from her shelter. Holes through solid oak instantly! Holes through men . . . Take her away if you do not believe. You will see! You will see!"

The man's superstition appalled Terues. He was especially sensitive to it because of the trouble irrational fears about his birthmark had caused him, and now this man's blatherings irritated him. Acros was so cultured—when one stood near the marble façades of the capitol. But all around it, in the pink mud houses where he had his shop, was ignorance and superstition that was easily manipulated by those who knew how. The culture was the face of Acros. But superstition was its soul. Damn that! He would take the stone, he decided, and he would begin carving it tomorrow. The shape was right for a large piece, and the geode . . . What could it do but increase his fame? At the moment he was totally certain of his powers.

He looked at Paros and at the dirty quarryman. "All right, Paros. Send this man with me to help me get it into my shop. You'll see something of this before long!"

Paros smiled once more. "I do not think so, Ter. I do not think so. You are too good."

Terues was old now, old and, tonight, more tired than he had ever been. He sat alone in the darkness of his shop, on a small stool next to his potting wheel with its massive granite flywheel. The only light came in smoky lashes from a single taper that added to the bare red glow from the furnace which Terues kept constantly fired. He was so tired. Phila had been with him here tonight, a beautiful young artist she was, a woman who laughed easily as light reflecting off her bare white shoulders. Terues had dared think that she was interested in him—he was, after all, the most famous sculptor in all of Acros even though he had not been seen at either Court or Guild for over twenty years. His pieces, from figurines to large frieze panels, graced the homes of all of Acros' nobility.

But Phila's interest in him was limited to a desire to learn Terues' unique modeling technique. With the force of her personality, and the promise of her body, she had attempted to part him from his secrets. When he had refused she left him, mocking him, calling him a stained relic. Terues touched the liver-colored oval birthmark on his cheek. The disappointment was bitter. He had expected it, certainly, after years of being treated with contempt, as if he was separate from the work he produced—yet, still he was disappointed, for he had allowed himself to hope that he could be wrong. Now, even that hope was gone.

Terues stood up stiffly. A little in front of him, near the center of the shop, a dusty sheet was draped over a pointed shape that was slightly taller than he was. It was the geode, which had stood where he and the quarryman had set it the day Paros had given it to him. He had attempted to begin work on it many times since then, whenever he was treated badly, or when he felt happy over a completed piece, whenever he felt his craft was either a solace or a joy to him. Yet he had always hesitated. The words of the quarryman would come back to him; there was always the doubt whether he really could carve the crystal. Now he went over to it. The sheet was gray and left a cloud of fine powder when he pulled it from the stone. Slowly, he ran his hand over its dirt-caked surface; the cool hardness was familiar to him now. Terues was tired, but he knew. It was time now for honesty, to begin at last to work for himself. He gathered his points and punches, his claws and rasps and stones, and his iron (for the crystal could be shaped by heat) slowly, knowing that whatever was inside that brown stone casing was calling to him.

She felt the strokes vaguely at first, then, as she sensed what was occurring, more definitely, sharp, heat-drawing, broadcasting a vibration that was absorbed throughout her body. She sensed him as a being of declining warmth, of cool extremities, though his thoughts were bright and very quick. She might have admired that had she not realized what was happening to her. As Terues worked eagerly, she was drawn out unwillingly from her slow slumber, from the peace that she had known by right for ages.

As her own thoughts moved more quickly she became angry. Quite quickly, she was able to discern his words, connect them to the occasional thoughts Terues displayed as he concentrated on his task. Alone in his room, surrounded by an aura of tapers (as distinct from his own aura, which she could also sense), he would mumble his intentions. "Ah, another chip of crystal," he would say, "another piece of your prison gone as I free you." Free her? He knew nothing about her; he was in fact whittling away at her very being!

She was being forced into a prison of his ideas, and she wanted to shout out, cripple him, stop him; but though the desire had risen, the ability to fulfill it had not. Her lack of control over the powers she did have was worse still. Periodically, the old man would bring a taper close to peer at a problem area, a flaw to be worked around or incorporated. The intense light would irritate her, the beams flicked out in anger, and she would feel his warmth descend quickly and remain still as he threw himself to the floor. Then he would laugh. "Yes, my love, you have missed me. You are angry, but I know you would never kill me." He was a fool. She would have killed him then if she could.

Terues, tireless in his drive now, continued working, and as he did she began to understand him better, to incorporate the terms of his world. She saw that the worse thing about him was not his foolishness—no, it was his vanity that fed her loathing of him. He professed his devotion increasingly as her form became more firmly linked to his intentions. To the degree that she became more what he wanted her to be his attachment became stronger. But as he shaped her, her own perceptions about him sharpened and improved. She saw that his love was only for what he was doing. What else could he love? He was alien, a brute with tools of cold steel.

He talked constantly. She pulsed softly, desperate in her desire to lash out once again, though that was still impossible. By either luck or skill he was careful never to excite her over that threshold again; thus, she could only wait anxiously for the time when the control would come to her. That would not be a hard wait, for patience had once been her very essence. Other faculties, the ability to sense him and her surroundings, were increasing, though as his work became finer the increases came in smaller increments. Soon, however, the power over the beams would be hers.

Until then, only a mistake on his part would grant her his death. Thus she was forced to listen to his chatter. Carefully sweeping yesterday's shards aside with his foot; he would come toward her, then sit, his brow glistening, his eyes alive with what he was doing. "Ah, you are so beautiful," he said, "like the untouched virgin on the dais in the capitol square who does not even lift a *finger* for modesty." Modesty! She was certain that modesty was the last thing he knew anything about. She wanted then to change her surfaces, spoil a whole day of shaping for him. But Terues kept the temperature too constant, and she could only shift her surfaces slightly. Her movements were to his will—the radiating heat of his iron was enough to force a contraction, however much she resisted, but not enough to activate her beams. Terues would laugh. "Ho, you are quite willing when persuaded, young lady!" She hated him all the more for the way he manipulated her so confidently.

"I am but an instrument for you," he claimed, and she had great difficulty understanding what he meant because she could not imagine that he was serious. He had, after all, formed her to his skills and his plans. Yet he claimed to have nothing to do with any of the process. She considered a mental bombardment —she was sure she could do it—but she rejected the idea. Her speech was his aim, she knew, the real desire held far back in the mind behind other, nobler motives. She could see that he really believed that if he were selfless enough and mindful of his craft, she would come to life for him. Obviously, he considered himself selfless enough, for he fully expected that she would. She saw in him a sad distaste toward his fellow creatures; there were memories of being treated very badly; Guild dinners to which he alone was not invited, memories which nurtured a tiny flame of revenge. Should such a subhuman attitude be rewarded? No. She would remain silent, for with the silence she could shape him as he had shaped her. She could crush him with it.

One day, after working ten hours polishing her with fine emery powder, he suddenly stood back, wiped his fingers quickly with a rag, then fell to his knees, announcing to her that she was beautiful, that he loved her. What damnable pride! What foolishness! The praise only meant that he expected thanks for releasing her. He knelt there, weeping in gratitude for having destroyed what she had been! And yet he thought the product of this destruction beautiful, reformed to the dictates of his own corrupt self-image. She saw that image, the tangled beard, white hair irregularly cropped close to the head, the face, dusted with powder through which the splotch on his cheek shone through with muted lividity. He turned from her and raised his hands in prayer:

"Dreyhu, I give thanks for the subtlety you granted my efforts. Though I am inclined to forsake the company of men, I wish I could find someone comparable to what has risen with your help from cold brown stone." He placed both hands over his face and once again wept in idiot joy.

She knew his words had been directed at no goddess other than herself. His gods were a reflection of his self-image, just as she was now. The prayer was merely a blatant appeal for her speech and it greatly ired her, though she also pitied him momentarily because of the emotional intensity which permeated his entire being. She thought again of killing him, for she was sure of that power now too. She even began to gather the necessary energy until she realized that any response she might make, even one which resulted in his death, would answer his prayer, satisfy him, prove to him that he had succeeded. She therefore renewed her determination to remain silent and made a special effort to cease the various pulsings of her body. He finally looked at her, the disappointment and hurt at not hearing her in his mind and on his face. It proved to her that there were other ways of killing men and that this was the best way. Let him strangle in his pride!

The old man still hoped, however, and was not daunted long. His eyes brightened after a time; of course, he was not yet worthy! "I have not yet shown you the depth of my feelings, Maia," he declared. Maia was his name for her; she despised the very vibrations of the sound. He came close enough to perceive his distorted image in each of her facets, touched them with a moist and trembling hand, with his wet lips. "I have waited for you, Maia." He ran suddenly to a dark corner of the shop and pulled a wooden sledge out from underneath a table. "Now you must see how I live. The lover knows the loved one's life intimately."

How he jostled her! He tipped her forward to get the sledge underneath, then pulled her back (with amazing strength for an old man) so violently that she feared she would break, become by his clumsiness utterly dissipated. What an array of beams would have greeted Terues then! But she was grateful they had not. She scarcely could have been conscious of his death. Now most of her awareness was directed toward controlling her pulses as the sculptor jolted her about the shop. She could barely keep her silence; worse, she realized that it signaled a change in her. Where once she had been content to simply exist, she now found a growing tendency to consider courses of action, a tendency fueled by an increasing quickness of temper. When he pulled her to the low bench that held his tools and ran to throw open the door ("Light," he said, "that is what one needs. Love needs light.") she could contain herself no longer. Her facets flashed violently out of pure frustration. To her disgust, Terues witnessed the display and loudly shouted his joy. She was furious, and determined that he never would see her respond to anything again. He tilted her toward the bench.

"The instruments that brought me to you, Maia." She sensed the barbaric cold metal fashionings of poor beings who desperately needed to surround themselves with what they had made, as if they needed proof and justification for their own existence.

Puffing with the effort, he turned her toward the small forge where coal nubbins still glowed dirty red. "This is where I formed the tools." Still fearing the beams, he was careful not to bring her too close. He grasped the leather bellows and demonstrated their use, blowing swirls of white ash about the room. "You see, the coals glow! Behind you you may have noticed the furnace. I've fired small models for every one of my figures there, save yours, Maia; you needed no model because you always were."

He kept on in this manner until he was exhausted by the effort and the joy. His confidence touched her in a small way. He was so certain that she would live (and she did live) and, if she lived, would love him. He stroked her again and again and would have lowered her to his pallet had he the strength. Instead, he lay down alone, gazing at her until her anger and frustration returned, exceeding all previous limits.

There was a noise from the door. A woman, one of Terues' fellow sculptors, entered the shop. Her name was Phila, and Maia could see that Terues feared something in her, the dark immediate vibrancy of her being which was almost overwhelming in its intensity. The difference between the two humans fascinated her. Terues stood up tiredly when he heard the light scuff of her sandaled feet over crystal dust. He was struck by the taper light which reflected in tiny points off Phila's hard, smooth fingernails.

Even in the murky light, Phila was amazed. "This is marvelous, Terues," she said. "Stunning! Fire-geode? You've finally done it."

Maia sensed the stiffening of Terues' manner as Phila moved closer to her, a total paranoia which colored him in blue transparent flame. "Why are you here, Phila?" he said weakly.

"Rumors. The Guild has waited a long time for you to work on this crystal."

"You've told them, I suppose?"

"No." Phila moved between the old sculptor and his statue, and Maia was quite amused by the tension between them, the stance and the gaming of their opposing aims. This did nothing, however, to staunch her anger at Terues. "No, not from me. Really, I have as little respect for the Guild as you, though I do take their crowns. No matter. I just came to question you on your methods." Slowly, she turned toward Terues, touching, even as she did so, a tiny flaw (part of her structure, not due to any failure on his part) with a long finger. Terues' nervous consternation gladdened Maia still more. But he maintained sufficient control to make a reply.

"There are ways, if one is cautious and does not try for too much at once. It forms itself quite readily." He attempted to inject more authority into his voice. "Phila, you know that my methods are my own. Certainly, the Guild knows that by now also." These were proud words. Maia knew that behind them was the notion that he was the only sculptor in Acros capable of doing anything with the techniques. Phila had vain thoughts of her own, of what she could have done with the crystal, that Terues had found her, perhaps, rather than carved her.

"Who at Court is to be blessed with this, then?"

"I have forsaken Court, as I forsook the Guild. I have been spit upon more than enough. This is mine, given to me alone."

Given! Phila apparently recognized this false modesty as well as Maia could. She was impressed by the human's perceptiveness. Phila laughed mockingly. "No doubt Dreyhu presented this creature to you in the dead of night as reward for all your suffering. Tell me, has it moved or spoken, as legends have it?"

Terues' panic was momentary, but it reminded Maia of his possessiveness, which she hated all the more for his rationalizing that she one day would possess him in return. It would not be a lie, he thought, to tell Phila what was certainly going to occur (though he was petrified of it not occurring).

"We understand each other, yes."

"Mmm." She saw an intention form in Phila's mind, and she would have agreed to it immediately had she been able to speak to her without Terues hearing also. Such was Maia's fury at the lie he had just told.

"Well, I ask you"—she smiled and licked her lips—"*both* of you, to reconsider your position. The Guild offers handsome compensation . . ." Phila left a lingering implication that somehow thrilled Maia as much as it disturbed Terues. A resigned stubbornness descended upon his brain.

"They could do nothing to exceed what I already have."

"Of course." She drew the hood of her cloak over her dark hair. "You are fortunate, aren't you?" Maia was glad to see her turn abruptly and leave. Phila's violent intentions made her realize fully the gap between what she was and what they were. The door closed. Terues blew out the taper, and comforting darkness shrouded her. Weakly, the old sculptor moved to his pallet, the concern he felt for his creation nearly making him ill. Maia relished that concern, and she scorned any thoughts suggesting possible abuse in Phila's hands. Weren't the fears ironic, since they violated the very tenets of the love he professed for her? She had supposed that love was an acceptance, that it was not a thing imposed upon objects of one's choosing. It implied no ownership, demanded no return, so how could she ever be taken from him? Truly, if he had loved her, would he not have left her in her slow, happy state?

Terues lay there, staring toward her in the darkness until his heavy sadness pulled him into a deep sleep filled with images that frightened him, images she did not understand. He thought himself trapped inside smooth places, or surrounded by circles of leering faces. The images were fascinating to her—at times she felt that she could almost comprehend their meaning. Perhaps she had been infected by her long contact with the human. Suddenly, she was unsure of herself and, turning away from Terues' dreams, attempted instead to merge with the darkness.

Soon she was confused, however, because it seemed impossible. Somehow, her essential patience was gone. Skittishly, she would seize at any vibration: the far-off howl of a dog, the clink of a collapsing ember, heat sources, or objects that drew heat away—anything that stimulated her. Still it was not enough. She began amusing herself with pulsing flashes in different complex rhythms that soon were strong enough to illumine the whole shop. She admired the patterns she created. Terues was still occupied with his dreams—he would not see—and after the long period of self-containment, it was very, very good.

The door opened slowly. Phila stood there, her expression triumphant and ghastly in the crystal glow that Maia damped almost immediately. She held a small oil lamp, and, after checking to see that Terues was asleep, she came to her and touched her surfaces with warm, faintly pulsing hands. She was, in fact, blood-full. The radiating heat, the internal vibrations which augmented the desire in her mind, confused Maia for a moment.

Phila whispered, "The old man was telling the truth. You do live! Speak, then. How were you formed?"

Maia considered. Phila knew even less of her than Terues did. Yet she still was angry, and the excitement of using the one power she had not yet employed had a certain attraction now. It would spite Terues. She formed the thoughts:

I live. Do not ask now how I came to be this way. *Bitter.*

Phila, in surprise, spilled hot lamp oil onto her bare thigh and nearly called out. Maia pulsed brief encouragement to her (which Phila interpreted as laughter) and then was assaulted by a succession of greedy images which poured from the woman, so different from Terues' gentler, more subdued thoughts. She was shocked.

"You know the thoughts of this selfish old man. He wants to keep you here alone, for himself. He wanted that for me once too. I know what you feel. I want more for a wonder such as you. I want to know you." She rested a cheek against the form of Maia's face.

I know you and I know Terues. You are alike in many ways.

Phila was annoyed and drew back slightly. But she was still determined.

"The old man is crafty. He can imprison you permanently here."

Maia floated up suddenly, moved a short distance away, pulsed her colors at Phila so that the light reflected in her dark shiny eyes. Her lips pulled away from long teeth.

"I tell you he can negate your power. There is a way, though. . . ." Maia saw now that Phila intended to murder Terues (oh, the satisfying purge of energy as by her own hand her rival breathed his last), then claim her as her own creation. It was worse than any of Terues' doting postures, yet it would free her from him. She spoke again.

I understand. Do what you will.

The communication was colored more with resignation than anticipation.

Phila was eager. "It can be done now."

Do not disturb the darkness. Tomorrow.

She injected this last thought with some force, enough so that Phila hesitated, turned toward her, and, when she was rewarded by a few hopeful pulses, she quickly left the shop.

The time that passed until Terues woke again seemed long, and there was little satisfaction in the revenge she had agreed to. She reminded herself that the sculptor's love was impossible, that he was attached not to what she was but to what he thought she was, to what he had made of her. As dawn came and she sensed the stirring all around the tiny building, it became increasingly difficult for her to renew her anger. She still thought Terues a fool, but she could see that, in comparison to Phila, he had a kindly nature. Although she had not attached much importance to it, she had seen in his thoughts that all the creatures who had wronged him before were possessed with vain pride far exceeding his. But Terues was, after all, her point of contact with all of these crippled human beings. With the weight of so much evil on his shoulders, it was fitting he should die. She could deal with others later.

Finally Terues rose stiffly, washed himself and urinated outside, then came back in and without so much as looking at her went to one of the tables and began carving on a small block of beeswax. She examined his mind curiously. It was empty of thoughts other than purely mechanical considerations of the craft involved. He was without intent or purpose, yet in a short time he fashioned a wax figure in her likeness, a fair likeness, he thought as he compared it to her. The form meant nothing (though it did seem harmoniously proportioned), but his method of working confused her profoundly. If he, without a real plan, had almost unconsciously copied her new form, then could he have done the same when he had reformed her originally? She did not know what to think.

He came to her at last and kissed her (she pulsed softly in surprise as he did so), then pulled her on the sledge over to a large tub of water on the other side of the shop.

"Maia, I wish you to see, as I once did, how your beauty called to me out of its formlessness." He tilted her over the tub as if he really believed that the sense organs he had fashioned for her could be better able to perceive what he was about to do. Then, rolling his sleeve up over his wasted arm, he plunged the wax figure into the water and stood back. "Watch, Maia. Watch yourself appear."

Slowly, the image came toward the surface, finally nudging the tensioned flatness, breaking out. A face appeared, a face like hers, like his, indefinite at first, then complete in an instant as the open air gave it solidity. Shoulders then, an arm, a finger, tearing away at the stillness of the tiny pool; all formed themselves as if gathered out of nothingness. But not out of nothingness, for the contours which appeared were determined by the essential wax figure. Terues stood her upright again and placed the dripping image onto the table.

"You see, that is how you came to me. I helped, nothing more. I had to bring out what you were, and now, even if you never speak, even if the legends are not true, I am honored to have helped, and I cannot help but love you. You are what you are —Phila could never see that. If you did live"—she saw his old last hope here, but without the confidence now—"I would humbly ask that you accept me in the same way, as I am." After seventy years of life, he was being as honest as he could be.

His demonstration and his words amazed her, and, more, she realized that his thoughts while speaking had been as still as his thoughts had been when he carved the figure. Now her silence was due to surprise, not spite. But he could not know that. The silence crushed him. His hope had rested on this appeal.

Weeping, Terues began pushing her toward a place he had

prepared for her in the corner of the shop, near the door, where shafts of sunlight from gaps in the ill-fitting doorjamb could touch her. Suddenly, Phila was there, her thoughts a hazy red. She hesitated momentarily, then pulled a slender dagger from a sheath beneath her cloak. Poisoned, Maia knew.

"Terues! In the name of the Guild, I claim this!"

The sculptor's fear was strong, but he diminished it by will. It was much too late for fear. "In your name, Phila," he said. "But she cannot be taken by you."

"Spotted fool! Your selfishness is your death!" She lunged toward Terues, who grasped her arm, though clearly, with his diminished strength, the struggle could not last long. Maia watched and suddenly realized that she was indeed Maia, a thinking being who could not allow this to happen. She acted without hesitation, employing her power for a new purpose. The beams seared the air in the room, and they were accurate. The dagger clattered away on the floor; Phila, pierced in the heart, fell at Maia's feet without time even to think of her betrayal. Terues understood. His eyes were still wet.

The voice trembled. "You speak?"

Yes. I accept you.

The Guild, gathered hungrily for news of Phila's mission, passed the time discussing how the marvel would be best used. The chatter stopped when the doors were thrown open. To wondering silence, Terues entered, dressed more finely than anyone could remember, the first time in twenty years that he had graced this chamber. He nodded ceremoniously. There was a gasp. Behind him came a woman of light, floating, moving fluidly (her limbs, her carved garments seemed to flow in the light breeze of their passage), flashing with such brilliance that all were forced to close their eyes. But even closed, an image remained, burned there, of a most beautiful face and the last moments of its strange movements. It was clear; she smiled at Terues. And in her arms she bore Phila, dead, as Terues regarded her with love.

Welcome, my gracious lord; welcome, dread queen;
Welcome, ye war-like Goths; welcome, Lucius;
And welcome, all. Although the cheer be poor,
'Twill fill your stomaches; please you eat of it.

—Shakespeare, *Titus Andronicus*

MYSTERY DIET OF THE GODS: A REVELATION

BY THOMAS M. DISCH AND JOHN T. SLADEK

Have you ever become suddenly quite ill after eating a single slice of buttered whole-wheat toast? Does your skin crawl inexplicably every time you see gigantic displays of "fresh" tomatoes? You are not alone! There are millions of others just like you who feel the same helpless rage when they see self-confessed Darwinians poisoning the wells of Education with their fairy tales about the so-called "Descent" of Man. According to those know-it-all Ph.D.s, the apelike hominids of the past were touched with some kind of magic wand—they call it Evolution!—and instantly they were transformed into today's useful citizens, poised at this moment on the very brink of Interstellar Space! Could anything be less likely? Who's kidding who, anyhow?

Now at last a few brilliant World Scholars are daring to challenge these fabrications. Erich von Däniken and others have established the basic groundwork of Truth on which others can begin to build: *viz.,* Our hominid ancestors were visited by "gods" from other planets, who mated with the apelike females (see Figure 1) to produce *Homo sapiens.*

Who were these extraterrestrial "gods"? Why did they come to Earth, breed a new race of intelligent creatures, and then mysteriously vanish? The answer is literally staring us in the face every time we sit down to breakfast, lunch, dinner, supper, and midnight snack. *Diet!*

What is more central to the very Mystery of Life than Diet? Who can deny that, as Albert Einstein probably said, "You are what you eat"? How true! Yet is it the *whole* truth? Perhaps we also eat what we are!

157

These two notions are but two sides of the same secret coin, as stated by William Makepeace Thackeray: "We have no wittles to eat, so we must eat *we.*" *(Ibid.)* Is Thackeray really suggesting cannibalism? And if not, how shall we account for the great Jonathan Swift's "Modest Proposal" in his book *The Portable Swift?* There Swift suggests that the Irish poor should kill and eat their own children. And Swift was a Protestant Divine! Are all three of these renowned sages—Einstein, Thackeray, and Swift—just "joking"? Are they crazy? Or had they stumbled on a fantastic secret, which would eventually cost all three of them their lives?

Recently, scientists taught a species of worm to crawl through an elaborate maze. (See Figure 2.) Then they cut up these "educated" worms and fed them to other worms. The new worms, who had never seen a maze before, calmly threaded their way through it without one false step. (One cannot help but think of the legend of Theseus and the Minotaur Ariadne.)

In the light of this all-important experiment, which we have never known one Establishment scientist to contradict, there is no need for theories of Evolution or the Transmigration of Souls to explain the origins of *Homo sap.* The truth is as simple as sandwiches: *The first diet of mankind was Man.*

Once one holds this key in one's hand, every door of History and of Ancient Legends may be opened with ease. Indeed, the most amazing thing is how long it has taken us to recognize this obvious truth, which seems literally to be staring at us from every newspaper headline and advertising billboard that we pass on the street, until one's impulse is to grab people and *force* them to look at the evidence!

Only consider these facts: The mightiest of Greek "gods," Cronos and Saturn, are said to have devoured their own children. (See Figure 3.) Since time began, Australian aborigines have performed a rite wherein they cut themselves and offer their blood to their children to drink—*in order to make them wise!* There are also many well-documented accounts of human sacrifices and blood-drinking ceremonies among the ancient Aztecs. Can this be merely "coincidence"?

If more proof be needed, what of this? The Greek hero Atreus, the Primal Chef, killed the children of his friend Thyestes, *boiled them in a cauldron,* and served them up at a special banquet. As Robert Graves explains: "When Thyestes had eaten heartily, Atreus sent in their bloody hands and feet, laid out on another dish. . . . Thyestes fell back, vomiting, and laid an ineluctable curse upon the seed of Atreus."

This legend has often been misinterpreted as pertaining to some taboo against parents (more advanced species) eating their children (less advanced species, the so-called "Under-privileged"). Poppycock! Thyestes' illness was the result of his children being *boiled in a cauldron.* No human nervous system can absorb unlimited traces of iron. The fact that Atreus realized this is shown by his trying to atone for his original sin by bringing in raw, pure flesh as a second course. For, as the ancients knew, it is only in eating raw meat (ambrosia) and drinking fresh blood (nectar) that vital essences can be transferred from eaten to eater.

Thus, the Arawak Indians of South America eat their victims raw, as did the sages of ancient Poland, the so-called Vampires. The same Diet Secret was known as well to the Moggadil of ancient Wales, who feasted on the raw kneecaps of their enemies, thereby gaining their strength. It is a well-known fact, documented in the *Protocols of the Elders of Zion,* that the medieval Jews (sages who preserved the hermetic doctrines of the space gods) made ritual—and probably very delicious—meals on Christian babies. The physicians of Pope Innocent III prescribed for him a daily dose of the fresh blood of three infants. At this point the "coincidence" theory begins to look very lame indeed!

Many ancient texts tell us precisely how autophagy originated. Hesiod, the earliest of the Greek poets, is thought to have personally known the extraterrestrial gods. He speaks of their secrets guardedly, as a "fable to the kings, who are themselves wise." The fable tells of a hawk who catches a nightingale, saying to him: "I shall make a meal of you if I wish, or set you free." At the end of his "poem," Hesiod reveals his true meaning with this warning: "You kings, mark this punishment well, even you: For the deathless gods are close among men. . . . *On the many-feeding earth there are thrice ten thousand immortal observers set there by Zeus to watch over mortal men.* They keep watch on judgments and evil deeds as they move, clothed in mist, all over the earth." *(Ibid.)*

Could any words be plainer? We were the food of 30,000 (thrice ten thousand) alien invaders. However, we weren't always helpless nightingales, as the distinguished British scholar Sir James Frazer demonstrates in *The Golden Bough*. After noting that the Cretans, at the festival of Dionysus, "tore a live bull with their teeth," he goes on: *"We cannot doubt* that in rending and devouring a live bull the worshippers of Dionysus believed themselves to be *killing the god, eating his flesh and drinking his blood."* In clear English, the mortals who had been mere Ambrosia revolted! The eaten became the eaters, and the worm turned!

As a direct consequence, our 30,000 hawks were indeed forced to clothe themselves in mist (possibly produced by the evaporation of "dry ice") and flee from the suddenly much smarter nightingales. Some went to Mexico, where they instituted their culinary practices on a truly grand scale. The eminent anthroposophist William H. Prescott tells us that in 1486 A.D., a year after the defeat of Richard III on Bosworth Field, at the dedication of the great temple at Huitzilopotchil, the prisoners reserved for the great banquet "were ranged in files, forming a procession nearly two miles long"! He asks—but neglects to answer—how the Aztecs could have dealt with this huge food surplus: "How could the remains, *too great for consumption in the ordinary way* [!?!?!], be disposed of, without breeding a pestilence in the capital?"

Archaeologists like Erich von Däniken have found the answer in the great Mexican pyramids. (See Figure 4.) Like those of Egypt, these gigantic edifices had a very practical purpose— *freeze-drying!* "This idea may sound Utopian," says Von Däniken, "but in fact every big clinic today has a 'bone bank' which preserves human bones in a deep-frozen condition for years and makes them serviceable again when required. Fresh blood—this too is a universal practice—can be kept for an unlimited time at minus 196° C., and living cells can be stored almost indefinitely at the temperature of liquid nitrogen. Did the Pharaoh have a fantastic idea which will soon be realized in practice?" *(Chariot of the Gods.* London: Souvenir Press, 1969, page 102. *Ibid. Q.E.D.)*

The answer must be a resounding *yes!* The flesh of mummies is so well freeze-dried that it is still delicious thousands of years

after it was put up! Think of the incredible know-how of those
pharaohs—how expertly the unsavory parts of the ambrosial
bodies were removed, how the cavities were then stuffed with
spices and neatly prepacked for the greater convenience of the
"gods." What we would give today for just one of the recipes!
The fact that sarcophagi depict the features of the deceased is
no longer an enigma to baffle Ph.D.'s (Ph.D. = Phony Dumb-
bell!). After all, don't *we* label our canned beans, frozen broc-
coli, etc., with appetizing pictures? (See Figure 5.)

Of course, prepacked foods are never as tasty as fresh. Perhaps for this reason the gods left Egypt and Mexico and settled
in the undersea city of Atlantis, somewhere near to the Shet-
land Islands. In the "legend" of *Beowulf* the human hero sets
off in a submarine to pursue the "god" called Grendel's Mother.
"For hours he sank through the waves. At last he saw the mud
of the bottom and all at once the greedy she-wolf who'd ruled
these waters for half a hundred years [i.e., since departing from
Egypt] discovered him." Grabbing him in her claws, she carries
him to Atlantis, which is described as "someone's battle-hall,
where the water could not hurt him, nor anything in the sea
attack him through the building's high-arching roof. A brilliant
light burned all around him." As for the Diet of the Atlanteans,
it's spelled out quite clearly, for this old chronicle begins with
a description of the extraterrestrial Grendel "coming to Herot
when Hrothgar's men slept, killing them in their beds, eating
some on the spot, fifteen or more at a time, and running off to
his *loathesome moor* [an obvious cryptogram of 'Atlantis' from
which only the 'n' and 'i' are missing] with another such sicken-
ing meal awaiting in his pouch." This pouch may have been the
trunk of a small, powerful car, probably a Volkswagen. A diving
expedition to the Shetlands would undoubtedly bring to light a
true Aladdin's cave of wonders. In fact, Atlantis and Aladdin's
cave are undoubtedly *one and the same!*

The one riddle remaining is: Why did Man, having tasted the
flesh of the gods and grown wise, regress into the corrupt vegetarian practices of his ape forebears? We see in the Book of
Genesis that eating roots, tubers, and fruit-pulp had always
been a temptation for the first humans. When the serpent
tempts Eve—poor half-simian creature that she was—with an
apple (or, more likely, a banana), he says: "In the day ye eat

thereof, then your eyes shall be opened, and ye shall be as gods."

How guileful! The serpent knew full well that a diet such as he is recommending would have just the opposite effect. We all know the tragic outcome of Eve's choice: Show an ape a banana and the rest, alas, is history. For one brief moment Man became a god—and then he slipped on the banana peel of his own deepest racial memories—and not just once but over and over again. First came the substitution of animal flesh for the real thing. Then the discovery of the abominable potato. After the rise of elaborate pastry chefs in the eighteenth century came the avowed vegetarianism of Percy Bysshe Shelley, George Bernard Shaw, and Adolf Hitler. Bloodless poetry led to cynical plays and on to a world plunged into hideous wars. (See Figure 6.) *All because Man has turned his back on his own flesh and blood.*

Is it too late to reverse this age-old tendency? No, by changing yourself, you can still change mankind! Here are four simple rules by which you can lead a life that will make you healthier and raise your I.Q. at least 20 points:

1. Boycott fruits and vegetables in any form.
2. All cereal products—rice, wheat, etc.—are out!
3. Banish coffee, tea, water, milk, and other unnatural beverages from your cupboards and refrigerators.
4. Use only meat substitutes, such as beef or venison, when you have no other recourse.
5. Insist on a plentiful, spontaneous Diet of the "Food of the Gods"—*Nectar* and *Ambrosia!*

On the public level—talk to your friends and neighbors. Show them the evidence—bit by bit. Ask them to read *Chariot of the Gods.* Then invite them to a dinner they'll never forget!

Finally, write to your congressman in Washington, D.C., asking for a return not only of the death penalty but of public human sacrifice. Let's make Thanksgiving a day to be truly thankful for by eating our own children, as did the original Pilgrim aliens.

If you want to *be* like gods, you've got to *eat* like gods. That's the Mystery of the Mystery Diet. It's still not too late for you to join the side of True Human Evolution and take your place in the great Garden of the Universe, where god eats god in an Eternal Cycle of glorious Diet!

It's up to *you!*

Suggested illustrations and captions:

Figure 1. (Venus di Milo) *Caption:* "Neanderthal woman. Note stooped, apelike posture, heavy jaw and narrow pelvic girdle."

Figure 2. (Photo of topiary maze) *Caption:* "Maze."

Figure 3. (Goya's painting of Saturn eating his children) *Caption:* "Goya's visionary rendering of the first contact between the 'gods' from Outer Space and Mankind."

Figure 4. (Any Mexican pyramid) *Caption:* "When explorers first opened the secret chamber of this Aztec pyramid, a light went on inside!"

Figure 5. (Any string of hieroglyphics) *Caption:* "Papyrus scroll found in the mummy-case of Im-hotep, a supermarket manager of the IVth Dynasty. It reads: 'Contains 100% Government-Inspected Ambrosia, with permitted preservatives.' "

Figure 6: (Crude "composite photo" of Shelley, Shaw, and Hitler) *Caption:* "Three vegetarians!"

"And isn't it strange," said the young lady, passing with startling suddenness from Sentiment to Science, "that the mere impact of certain coloured rays upon the Retina should give us such exquisite pleasure?"

—Lewis Carroll, *Sylvie and Bruno*

IN CHINISTREX FORTRONZA THE PEOPLE ARE MACHINES OR, HOOM AND THE HOMUNCULUS

BY MICHAEL BISHOP

In the empery of Chinistrex Fortronza on the planet Blaispagal, Inc., the people were machines. For as long as anyone could remember the people had been machines, as had the animals in the whirring forests, and the fish in the lubricating seas, and the birds that hummed and chittered in Blaispagal, Inc.'s electric air: all were perpetually wound, spontaneously self-repairing automata.

Maybe once there had been organic creatures on this world of cybernetic ascendancy, but archaeology was not a science of any repute among her mechanical citizens; and if beings of blood, bone, and mortal flesh had ever existed here, they lay fossilized and forgotten in the faulted, striated strata of beautiful Blaispagal, Inc.'s ferriferous, red earth: time-torn architectures of Death, a condition of which the Blaispagalians knew almost nothing since for them the ultimate entropic disaster was merely a repairable malfunction. Tap into the circuitry of the emperor (who in Chinistrex Fortronza was called the Parmalee), and *voila! mon frère,* you are well again.

By religion, then, the people were deists, for God of course was the transcendent Watch Maker who had wound them all up and then benignly left them to their own devices. Organizationally (you and I would say "politically"), in each and every one of the planet's several autonomous corporate bodies, the people were mechanostatists believing in the divine right of 'chines and therefore practicing a pert, ta-pocketa-pocketa obeisance to whichever august automation had evolved to a probity of operation and control so *dependable* that it never, no, never, broke down.

In Chinistrex Fortronza this esteemed entity was the two-meter-tall, artificial bird of paradise Pajetric Stat, Parmalee to More Than Half a World and Cybernetic Wonder Universally Unparalleled.

Of hammered gold and gold enameling was the Parmalee Stat mainly made, and for a mild eternity he had sat on the highest bough of the golden throne-tree at the bottom of a glass-and-aluminum shaft in the minareted Command Center of Chinistrex Fortronza, alertly attuning himself to the pulses and pistonings of his empery, showily cantilevering his silver-wimpled wings and issuing melodious decrees in every variety of computerese and mechanical patois known to his people. Now and again, in his function as priest as well as parmalee, Pajetric Stat would lift a series of formulae to the erstwhile Watch Maker who had wound them all up. It was a happy and well-regulated existence that the Parmalee both monitored and embodied, this monarchial bird of paradise.

From the many other corporate emperies of Blaispagal, Inc., came an influx of automata—efficiency units, robo-aestheticians, optical scanners—to tour the facilities of Chinistrex Fortronza, and to time-share audiences with Pajetric Stat. From the corporations of Datcoa, Selestron, Randland, Ampide, Bzz, and Divroid Phic came these representatives, and once home again each one of them unreeled printout upon printout extolling the virtues of Chinistrex Fortronza: from the climate control, to the exquisite synchronization of the populace, to the opulent dependability and near-omniscience of Pajetric Stat. Indeed, their praises hummed. Upon occasion, so mightily had these visits worked upon the cluck-a-clucking emissaries, their eulogies ratcheted out in rhymed dactylic hexameters. . . .

Oddly enough, however, the visitors reserved their lengthiest comment and most puzzled praise for the only denizen of Chinistrex Fortronza that the Parmalee, even as Most High Regulator and Monitor of his people, had never felt pulse from or fed energy to: the Homunculus.

The Homunculus?

In some reports this machine was called, in Blaispagalian equivalencies, the Mennikin, the Dwarveter, or the Orangouman. But most often, the Homunculus.

Said the messages sped from synapse to synapse through the microminiaturized neuristors of Pajetric Stat, "But of all the marvels of Chinistrex Fortronza the most remarkable is the Homunculus." Over and over again among the visitors' relayed printouts this sentiment occurred, provoking something vaguely like a glitch in the Parmalee's heretofore glitch-free systems. Indeed, his cryotrons overheated. But the only outward sign of annoyance or possible (minuscule) malfunction he made was an overly showy cantilevering of his silver wings and sapphire-eyed tail, which, the hall being empty, no one witnessed.

What was the Homunculus? The accounts indicated that this machine, who dwelt secretly in the private forest, or paradise, of the Parmalee, mimicked to perfection the attributes of a strange consciousness that was neither digital nor analogical.

Although an automaton like the other inhabitants of Blaispagal, Inc., the Homunculus had the behavioral capacity to suggest *emotion:* it could *laugh,* piteously *keen,* yea, even shed *tears.* Much was made of the affective nature of this last operation, of how the visual perception of the Homunculus's tears— lachrymal gemstones produced at will in polymer-coated ducts behind its "eyes"—could throw off your rheostats or make your flywheels falter.

Even so, the servitors in Parmalee Stat's wooded and crystal-hung paradise often paused in their labors to register the wail of the Homunculus, or, distance seldom being a let to the high-powered robo-rangers, to record the magnitude of brilliance of one of its glinting tears. Swinging through the dark, dark park the Homunculus would flash on the sensor units of the rangers and disappear. Sometimes its ululating keen lingered in undulant lambency on their stomach oscilloscopes. Its presence, though, lingered even longer than that, a haunting quasi-glitch. . . .

The Homunculus, you see (and this is information not even the emissaries of Datcoa, Selestron, Randland, Ampide, Bzz, and Divroid Phic gleaned during their visits), was the immortal representative of a single generation of machines programmed in secrecy before the decline and fall of organic consciousness on Blaispagal, Inc., when in fact the planet had been unincorporated and called by such names as Azúl, Organdy Dancer, Sweetflame, and other equally mawkish, nonmechanical tags. This may account for some of the Homunculus's strange accouterments. Tiny copper bristles overlay the *head, shoulders,* and bandy *arms* of the Homunculus, giving it what no other machine or electronic unit in Chinistrex Fortronza, or anywhere else, possessed: a shaggy, copper-colored *fur.* Moreover, it had a totally plastic (in several senses) *face,* which it could contort, wrinkle, or stretch when an esoteric internal mechanism triggered the proper stimuli for these responses. In addition, it suffered a built-in *grief* for its extinct and dimly remembered creators, a grief that occasioned its poignant keening and compelled it to avoid the congregating places of later species of machine.

The origin of the Homunculus millennia in the past, then, and its deliberate solitariness explain in part the Parmalee's ignorance of its existence; the awe of the Chinistrex Fortronzans before so odd and illogical, albeit wonderful, a phenomenon must explain the Parmalee's remaining so long in the dark. But now Pajetric Stat had been enlightened—cruelly enough, by foreigners.

"What is this Homunculus, this Mennikin, this Dwarveter, this Orangouman?" he wondered for the 10^{29}th time. "What is this marvel that is the 'most remarkable' in Chinistrex Fortronza? Am I to learn about my own corporate empery from the printouts of traveling robo-aestheticians?"

Pajetric Stat tapped into the bowels of his right-hand wing-rider, the computer on wheels RunAbout Most High. It was RunAbout Most High's function to compile and store lists of all the empery's employees, complete with duty descriptions, vital statistics, and maintenance records. He also performed for the Parmalee whatever command responsibilities required mobility.

Barrel-shaped and tentacled, RunAbout delighted in busybodying from place to place piping out pitch-coded instructions and tweaking the exposed console bulbs of the Command Center chamber-aides. If anyone but the Parmalee ventured to tap into him RunAbout ostentatiously lit up a buzzer-accompanied message-panel spelling out *"Tilt!"*: a response designed to minimize impertinent feedback.

Tapped the Parmalee, "What can you tell me, RunAbout, about a machine called the Homunculus? Courtesy tapes from recent visitors inform me that it can laugh, lament, and let fall tears; that, indeed, it is the 'most remarkable' marvel in all Chinistrex Fortronza."

RunAbout Most High scanned his integrated innards. "No info bit regarding a mechanism and/or solid-state unit registered as the Homunculus, Your Parmalee. . . . Zizizi, click, re-scan. . . . No, Your Paradisiacal Birdship, no bits, no info, no news."

"But it exists, RunAbout, it nevertheless exists."

"Zizizi, click, re-scan: I don't see how you can be so certain, Your Parmalee. All my components tell me otherwise." Sententiously RunAbout appended, "Digesting as empirical truth the printouts of ill-constructed foreigners is seldom an energizing pastime."

"However, RunAbout, I have one such printout with the imprimatur of the Mechanarch of Divroid Phic, and *his* structural integrity I do not doubt. The story must be true. Therefore, I wish that the Homunculus, whatever it may be, appear before me this evening at 2100 hours in the well of the throne-tree to laugh, lament, and let fall tears, that Pajetric Stat escape an ignorance unbecoming to your Parmalee. Go, RunAbout, and find this 'marvel.' "

For a short period RunAbout Most High ran about, mostly out of mild mechanical trauma: he realized that should he fail to fetch back the Homunculus by 2100 hours Pajetric Stat would cut the juice to every one of the automata and servitors in the Command Center. Indeed, the Parmalee might even induce a punitive infestation of ferric oxide in their capacitors and diodes! "Zizizi, click, re-scan," murmured RunAbout Most High, inefficaciously. He then began to roll back and forth through the air-conditioned tunnels of the Command Center in search of the Homunculus; to levitate up and down the glass-walled, hologramic storage-shafts.

By happy and not altogether random chance RunAbout encountered in the vestibule of the Center a robo-ranger from the

Parmalee's paradise: this simple servitor, ycleped Smoky, was there seeking a replacement for a burnt-out cathode-ray tube. One too many times had Smoky's stomach oscilloscope reverberated to the keening of the bandy-armed, rubber-faced Homunculus. "But I no mind," it said in husky, pidgin FORTRAN; "The Homunculus scream just so, you know, it drop-drop the diamond tears, I warble-hum inside. Is really a Homunculus, O RunAbout Most High; is really, you know."

"Robo-ranger," RunAbout said, "lead me to the Homunculus. Do you so, and I will give you a stationary installation beneath the throne-tree of Pajetric Stat, from whence you may witness the majestic wimpling of the underside of his many-eyed tail."

"Gracious thanks," said Smoky.

Into the forest of the Parmalee's paradise they ventured together, along with a retinue consisting of an omnivorous vacuum cleaner called Univac, a musical synthesizer answering to Morp, and a pair of nameless mobile generators.

The woods burped, burbled, and roared with static.

At 1940 hours RunAbout Most High registered a distant wailing and Smoky picked up the Homunculus's telltale spoor: a trail of tears. This they followed, Univac sucking up same, and at 1952 hours were rewarded by a glimpse of their elusive prey. Morp the Synthesizer, programmed to emulate the dwarveter's every lamentation, keened and keened, burbling a bit more electronically than did the Homunculus itself. Even so, the Homunculus paused to record this untoward and imperfect aping of its audible grief, and at 2009 hours the party from the Command Center drew up beneath the living conifer, draped with pastel filaments of quartz, in which their prey now resided, curious mechanism that it was.

It stared down, they stared up, and a chunk of moon evermore in synchronous orbit with Blaispagal, Inc., littered the paradise's shaggy trees with starlike sparklings.

"O Homunculus," RunAbout Most High began, the sensor screens of his retinue all lifted to the thing above them, "Parmalee Pajetric Stat wishes you to laugh, lament, and let fall tears for him." Even as he made this request, RunAbout flooded his own information centers with questions: How could so ungainly, so loosely bisymmetrical a machine fulfill any purpose whatever? Of what utility were laughing, making high moan, and shedding gemstonelike tears? In the lineaments of the Homunculus, in fact, slept something repellent, something invidious to good organization and efficient command. At least on first impression.

But then, contorting its lugubrious, plastic face, the Homunculus chortled sadly, shaped with its crazy speaker unit a howl much purer than Morp's, and littered the ground with a rain of worthless, utterly worthless, diamonds. The spectacle, all inutile as it was, sent the logic circuits of RunAbout Most High pleasantly awry: "Zizizi, click, re-scan." Smoky's oscilloscope burned out another tube, but somehow the loss was a psychomechanical reward. Univac hiccuped, happily hiccuped, and Morp fell awe-strickenly silent.

RunAbout implored the Homunculus to return with them to the Command Center; he set Morp the Synthesizer off as a sort of guide-piper to their crew.

And, unpredictably enough, the Homunculus followed: a squat, heavy shadow swinging through the sparkles cast down by Blaispagal, Inc.'s seemingly stationary moon.

By 2100 hours, just as the Parmalee had directed, the orangouman was standing under the throne-tree in the control shaft of the Command Center: body hunched, arms hanging, head thrown unkemptly back to scan the artificial bird of paradise who had summoned it. Once, the Homunculus recalled (an archetypal hum coursing from switch to switch in its belly), creatures more like itself—aye, *creatures*—had commanded its time, punched in its duties, applauded its creaturely responses. A familiar grief then began coursing in its innards, a counterpoint to the hum of memory. How good, though, to be commanded again, even if by a digital intelligence rather than an organic one.

"If you would, Homunculus," the Parmalee said from aloft, cantilevering wings and tail, "do for me as you did for RunAbout and the others: laugh, make moan, and show me these things called tears."

And so, spreading its copper-haired arms as if to embrace the old grief that powered it, the Homunculus did. With this exception: its laugh was a sob, it could not this night bypass the ancient templates of its programmed sorrow.

As for Pajetric Stat, in a detonation of wonder he realized the correctness of the printouts of the emissaries of Blaispagal, Inc.'s other corporate emperies, and for the first time in the presence of another machine he released through the speaker in his golden beak that complicated, mathematically intense, baroque concerto he had long ago composed to help him cope with moments of electronic overload. The glass-and-aluminum control shaft echoed with this melody, and the Homunculus, humbled, felt itself well repaid for its own brief performance. It had heard the Parmalee sing!

The next day Pajetric Stat permitted the other calculators, servitors, and chamber-aides in the Command Center to audit through telemetry and time-sharing the relayed talents of the Homunculus. Closed-circuit holovision let them optically apprehend the dwarveter's tears.

And from that day forward the Homunculus was as famous in Chinistrex Fortronza as Pajetric Stat himself. Ordinarily staid machines began purposely simulating "emotion": they laughed (so to speak), wept, and burbled in premeditated, ratchety runs up and down the chromatic scale, some even lapsing into dodecaphonic feedback squeals that blew fuses, shorted out sockets, and larruped up work schedules. The Parmalee tolerated this—indeed, he never once threatened to cut off their juice—because when his machines *weren't* homunculing around, they performed with a pizzazz and verve unprecedented in the history of the Command Center. Besides, none of them had yet managed to manufacture tears, which were, after all, potentially computer-room-cluttering.

The robo-rangers in the Parmalee's paradise elected the Homunculus their official mascot: The Machine Who Weeps Starlight, they dubbed him. (As cathode-ray tube repairs continued to rise, a minor efficiency unit in the Command Center determined that the forest servitors didn't need oscilloscopes anyway.)

RunAbout Most High installed in himself an entire bank of circuitry devoted to digesting and responding to queries about the new Corporate Resource of Chinistrex Fortronza: the Homunculus. Less and less often did his message-panel buzz out *"Tilt!"* when an auxiliary unit of some sort tapped into him for advice or general amplification.

Morp the Synthesizer composed, in an accessible binary code,

a temper-balancing ditty entitled "Homunculi, Homuncula."
Two days later the whole empery was humming it compulsively
on ordinarily unused channels of private communication.

Then, one day, there arrived at the Command Center a large
aluminum box with a number of holes bored into each one of
its six faces. So unusual was this box that the machines that
brought it into the vestibule didn't even notice the emissary—
who looked like an abbreviated lightning rod surmounted by a
frosted glass globe—who had come along with it. RunAbout
Most High was summoned, and when he appeared he demanded of the offloaders, "What is this obstruction? Why are
you mucking about?"

"I am the Mechanarch of Divroid Phic's messenger," the
globe-surmounted lightning rod averred. "And I have brought
a gift for your illustrious Parmalee. Please usher me in to him."

"Here is a terminal," said RunAbout, gesturing to a wall console, "from which you may call in your request or message."

"No," the emissary said firmly. "I must see the Parmalee, as
it were, in the very metal. So the Mechanarch, Pajetric Stat's
counterpart, has commanded me."

Since it could not be got around, RunAbout Most High ordered the box trucked into the control well and accompanied
the visitor from Divroid Phic to the base of the throne-tree.
There the gift was uncrated. "What a strange machine," said
the Parmalee, cocking his golden head and gazing down.

"It is not a machine at all, Your Parmalee," said the emissary,
and at once both Pajetric Stat and RunAbout Most High realized that the *thing* they were looking at resembled—in almost
every way but its utter want of copper-bristle fur—the Homunculus who, for the past twenty-odd fiscal periods, had captured
the neuristors and vacuum tubes of the empery. Oh, yes, another difference: the gift was conspicuously *more* misshapen
than the Homunculus. And there it stood at the bottom of the
well, all unadorned and shivering.

"Not a machine?" Pajetric Stat said.

"Then what?" RunAbout Most High inquired.

With their gift blubbering to itself like a small vat viscously
boiling mud, the emissary from Divroid Phic explained that
upon first hearing of the Homunculus in Chinistrex Fortronza,
his Mechanarch had decreed a crash program to develop a

machine with similar capabilities. Computer research, however, had suggested that this might best be done not through exclusively cybernetic methods but instead by the application of the principles of a new science which D.Ph.'s Chief Engineer ADMA 7 had cryptically tagged "bionics." "What is this *bio?*" the Mechanarch had asked; and ADMA 7, unable to communicate this concept adequately, had tapped out, "Trust me, Your Dependableness," and proceeded to discard from his team's researches even the familiar and comprehensible group of studies signaled by the suffix *-onics*. To create a homunculus on a par with the wonderful one of Chinistrex Fortronza, ADMA 7 said, would require not something more but something other. . . .

"Although no one but he fully understands it," the frosted globe continued, pulsing—at least to Pajetric Stat's divination— a bit maniacally, "ADMA 7, who is a genius by virtue of a serendipitous foul-up in the initial stamping of his circuitry, discovered a whole new complex of systems and sets: *biology!*"

The Parmalee and RunAbout exchanged tiny surges of uncoded current: the morpheme *bio*, carrying no more semantic freight for them than it had for the Mechanarch of Divroid Phic, struck them as somehow improper.

Then the frosted globe began telling them, in a monologue that was no doubt pre-recorded, how ADMA 7 had enlisted the aid of *nucleic acids* in his researches; how he had plumbed the *prebiotic formation of carbohydrates and fats;* how he had effected the *polymerization of amino acids into proteins;* how he had isolated the specific functions of the acid *glycine;* and how, finally, he and his team had *animated* all this alien material into systems which were entirely independent of mechanical or electronic impetus.

The end result was the thing that now hunkered and shook, rubber-necked and whimpered at the base of Pajetric Stat's throne-tree: "Organic intelligence," the emissary said.

Emanations from the gift gave the Parmalee's olfactory sensors pause, but since they were so seldom exercised his Paradisiacal Birdship was not offended.

"This is as far as ADMA 7 and his team could take their experiments," the visitor continued, his dogmatism at last mediating into a nice, mechanical humility. "In comparison to the Homunculus of Chinistrex Fortronza it is a sorry specimen, a clumsy and insulting mock-up—but the Mechanarch, out of respect for you, apologizes for its shortcomings and hopes that you will find it diverting in moments of programmed off-time.

"Its name is Hoom, and it runs, disgustingly enough, on chlorophyl patties, H_2O, and internally produced fuels that ADMA 7 has labeled its *neuroses*. We have given you a supply of each." With that, the emissary took his leave.

What now? the Parmalee wondered, and RunAbout Most High hurried after the globe-surmounted lightning rod to give him a seemly and machinely send-off: "Zizizi, click, re-scan."

Hoom, its organic intelligence alert to the departure of its guardian, commenced to lament and let fall tears. Although an involuntary scan revealed that the tears were salt water rather than gemstones, Pajetric Stat found this a refreshing change. Hoom's tears would evaporate; the Homunculus's had to be swept up. Then the Mechanarch's gift began to crack its crimson knuckles, pound its breast plates (which were neither metal nor plastic, the Parmalee divined), and batter its hairless head against the lowest branches of the throne-tree. Here was a grief at least three exponents more violent and demonstrative than that the Homunculus usually manifested. The effect on the Parmalee, then, was by just that degree intensified. No complex concerto escaped his speaker unit, but instead a shrill, high whistle as strange as the creature that had provoked it. It surprised Pajetric Stat.

Also surprised, Hoom left off its heartfelt histrionics. Hoom fell silent. Then Hoom laughed; ca-ca-cackled like a battery of breaking console lights.

Not often or for very long did the real Homunculus laugh: its programmed grief always overcame it. Metering his reaction, Pajetric Stat discovered that the novelty of Hoom's laughter pleased him, registered well on those calibrating mechanisms arrayed like clockwork inside his golden breast. Quite a while, after all, had gone by since the Homunculus's first appearance in the control well, and the edge had gone off everyone's appreciation of the original dwarveter's still inexplicably affecting talents. Morp's "Homunculi, Homuncula" had long since given way, on the private channels of Chinistrex Fortronzans, to a Muzak melody entitled "Do Not Staple, Spindle, or Fold." A population cyberlutionarily evolved to cope with tedium and routine had developed a taste for variety; likewise, the Par-malee.

The day after Hoom was delivered, Pajetric Stat called the Homunculus into the control well, confronted him with the organic consciousness incarnate in the misshapen creature from Divroid Phic (whose resemblance to itself the Homunculus did not fail to detect), and asked that the two laugh, lament, and let fall tears *together*.

This was not a success. Both attempted what was asked, but the Homunculus could not sustain its own laughter nor synchro-nize its keening with that of the obstreperous Hoom. And when the mechanical dwarveter began producing tears, Hoom, face streaked with wetness, began picking them up, rattling them together, and thrusting them up at the fluorescents overhead to make them sparkle.

The sparkling made Hoom laugh, and the performance, come full circle (assuming the circle somewhat oblate), there-fore broke down: *"Tilt!"* RunAbout Most High wasn't even around to signal the breakdown with a buzz. Hoom, though, kept laughing at random intervals and the Parmalee emitting his shrill, appreciative whistle, so that the Homunculus, grief for its millennia-dead creators switching into personal channels, left the Command Center, swung back into the depths of Pajet-ric Stat's paradise, and disappeared.

No one noticed, although in the crystal-hung woods the robo-ranger Smoky (RunAbout Most High, you see, had failed to come through with a Center-based sinecure) again picked up the familiar ululations of the Homunculus and felt, down where its oscilloscope had used to be, a pleasant heat.

When it was discovered back in the Command Center that the real orangouman had left them, an epidemic of indifference broke out.

And why not? The Parmalee—recording, amplifying, and broadcasting the capabilities of Hoom to every unit in the com-plex—had given his machines a multitude of new concepts to store and toy with. Prime among these was the phenomenon of organic excretion, since Hoom *sweated, eliminated,* and, in oc-casional fits of wall-banging passion, *bled.* It was true that the people of Blaispagal, Inc., gave off heat and light, but about Hoom's (perhaps) analogous processes there flitted an aura of the elemental and earthy, as if before the elements had been numbered and the earth refined. The Homunculus was forgotten. Now the computer consoles, the servitors, the chamber-aides—all the corporate automata—spent their leisure simulating Hoomlike *waste matter* and *smells*. Too, they engaged in cross-circuited powwows the purpose of which was to derive a formula for credible electronic laughter.

In praise of the organic homunculus, Morp composed a song adroitly punning on computerese grammar: "Who Is Subjective, Hoom Is Objectionable" (in rough translation). The lyrics made a point of contradicting the title:

> Who is subjective,
> Hoom is objectionable.
> But whoever's selective
> Finds Hoom delectable.

This ditty quickly replaced "Do Not Staple, Spindle, or Fold" on the hit parade tapes of the empery. In gratitude and joy RunAbout Most High presented Morp the Synthesizer with its own independently operable powerpak.

And for the next five revolutions of Blaispagal, Inc., Hoom, its novelty undiminished, its affective capabilities intact, chittered impudently in Pajetric Stat's throne-tree, chortled freely in the echoing command shafts, chased wantonly among the tunnels of the complex. Its fame was assured, its position secured.

Meanwhile, beyond the Center, the Homunculus of old—the *real* Homunculus—made high moan for whichever servitors in the Parmalee's paradise might be listening and littered the ground with gemstones. It was half in love with easeful malfunction, but nevertheless continued to self-repair.

Then one day, right there in the control well, Hoom collapsed and did not get up. The Parmalee had seen Hoom turn itself off before, often for hours on end while its various internal and psychomechanical units, he supposed, revitalized themselves. But this was different. This was the result not of a revitalization but of a bankload of breakdowns.

Two X-ray-equipped scanning machines found alien, apparently inimical particles of a microscopic nature in Hoom's *bloodstream* (this being its curious analog of a machine's electronic circuitry), and the larger of the robo-diagnosticians said to Pajetric Stat, "Hoom continues to function at automatic, non-conscious levels, Your Paradisiacal Birdship, but is still very close to terminal shut-down."

For the duration of an entire fiscal period, thirty slow rotations of the planet, Hoom lay inert and incommunicative beside a monitoring console in a subsidiary tunnel of the Command Center. It dwelt, said the monitor, in a hinterland between *on* and *off*. Intravenously, Level-1 mechanics conscripted for "bio duty" plied the malfunctioning creature with liquefied chlorophyl patties and lactase-spiked lubricants. Who knew precisely what would work, what fail?

During Hoom's maddening dormancy a failure of another sort captured the attention of Pajetric Stat: the gross corporate product of Chinistrex Fortronza, for the most recently concluded fiscal period, had fallen below that of Divroid Phic for the first time since . . . who could remember? Yea, the C. Fortronzan g.c.p. was being challenged even by such lightweight emperies as Selestron and Bzz! Efficiency had fallen off, the pizzazz and verve of times past had degenerated into a mopy, glitch-ridden languor. Why? Easy to say: Hoom was terminating, and the citizens of Chinistrex Fortronza had registered the fact in all its computer-counted ramifications.

What or who, with Hoom gone, would touch them in those enigmatic recesses—recesses neither digital nor analogical—that they'd not been previously conscious of? Who or what would restore them to peak temper and dependability?

The answer came at once to Pajetric Stat (as it must surely have already come to you): only the Homunculus, only the Homunculus.

But could the Homunculus be enticed from its self-imposed banishment in the eerily neat depths of the Parmalee's paradise? Had it perhaps been *hurt*—the Parmalee struggled with the abstruseness of this notion—by their attentions to Hoom? Yes; most certainly. As a consequence, had it manufactured a quantity of *pique*? Again, most certainly. Logic confirmed the undeniable likelihood of both possibilities. And sending out RunAbout Most High, Smoky, Univac, and Morp the Synthesizer to retrieve the Homunculus would hardly work a second time.

Once bidden, once sly.

Hoom continued operable a second fiscal period, and a printout from Divroid Phic's ADMA 7, in response to pleas for cooperative research on the problem, said that the organic homunculus would most likely . . . *die:* the same thing had happened, in time, with all their other decanted intelligences.

The term *die* was then explained in a sheaflet of printouts designed as a footnote to ADMA 7's initial reply; the footnote included analogies, graphs, experimental examples. Pajetric Stat, scanning them, could not help applying these statistics and prophecies to the g.c.p. of Chinistrex Fortronza: down, down, and *dead.* Soon even tiny Bzz, ruled, as rumor had it, by an abacus, would be capable of becoming a majority shareholder in their empery.

The Parmalee's wings ratcheted up, ratcheted down in overwarm unison, light playing upon them with unhealthy incandescence.

At the end of the second fiscal period there occurred a drop in the g.c.p. commensurate with Hoom's monitored decline. About this time RunAbout Most High disappeared from the Center: he had defected, it was later learned, to Ampide. . . .

"Dear, dear Homunculus," Pajetric Stat murmured to himself, "when will this irrationality and glitchiness end?"

Would Hoom recover?

Would the Homunculus return?

As the Watch Maker of all Blaispagalians would have it, Hoom *died.* The last pulse beat went out of the creature, tiers of telemetering equipment went fuzzily blank.

When the Parmalee informed his people of the organic homunculus's *death,* work stopped altogether. Morp the Synthesizer broadcast over the entire empery a single reverberating, grief-filled chime. Servitors and sedentaries stopped humming long enough to record the protracted *bong* from Morp's woofers and to say to each other, "Yes, it's true: the bell tolls for Hoom."

The organizational structure of Chinistrex Fortronza was disintegrating; and contemplating this from the isolation of the control well, from the topmost branches of his throne-tree, Pajetric Stat, fighting overload, warbled the whole of his complex concerto to an empty room. Or so he thought.

When he looked down again, he saw the Homunculus beneath him, diamonds poised on its cheeks like glass commas. Quietly, the dwarveter began to weep—wept because it had forgotten how to laugh, wept because it had again heard the Parmalee sing. Almost at once Pajetric Stat overcame his surprise and switched on the mechanisms that would relay the sights and sounds of the joyously lamenting Homunculus to all the citizens of his empery: no time to lose, no time to lose. That done, the Parmalee addressed the Machine Who Weeps Starlight in terms of genuine gratefulness and affection.

"Long, long ago, Homunculus, I should have turned Hoom out, I should have sent it back to the Mechanarch of Divroid Phic."

"Not so, Your Paradisiacal Birdship, for Hoom served you well and would still be doing so if it had not been who and what it was: an organic entity. Its misfortune was greater than our own, the misfortune of mortality. Do not revile it either for temporarily replacing me or for so inconsiderately terminating. I am back now, and coming and going as I please, I will continue to influence—by my bitter laughter, my lamentations, and my lachrymal displays—the hidden sensibilities of our people. I will touch the mortal in them that lies unsuspected and impetuous under their immortal skins. And under yours, too, my Parmalee."

"So be it," said Pajetric Stat.

And so the Homunculus did, its grief for its dead creators an incentive and an inspiration for its fellow citizens. In the very next fiscal period Chinistrex Fortronza recovered its cybernetic leadership of the corporate emperies of Blaispagal, Inc., and a press printout from Ampide reported that a pack of indigenous robots, unprogrammed primitives, had cannibalized RunAbout Most High for parts and bartered these for sturdier varieties of scrap metal. Upon receiving this news, the machines in the Command Center unanimously elected the Homunculus to the late RunAbout's position, and the Homunculus, a bit against expectations, accepted.

And everyone functioned happily ever after: literally.

On the other hand, poor dead Hoom was the only citizen of Chinistrex Fortronza who ever went to a paradise other than the Parmalee's coniferous and crystal one. Or who, to be fair, needed to go there.

Zizizi, click, re-scan.

The centuries had already stopped
believing the literal truth of such tales
when they began to scribble these
hyperboles across the sky. . . .

—Tom Disch, "The Constellations"

LEGENDS FROM "THE CHESHIRE CAT"

BY ENRIQUE ANDERSON IMBERT

Translated from the Spanish by Isabel Reade

IN THE LAND OF EPHEMERA

The chronicle is from the ninth century, but the events it recounts are much older.

The knight Guingamor departed in search of the Land of the Blessed, whose inhabitants—according to an Irish monk—did not age or aged only slightly and lived eternally or for several centuries. All the visitors would have to do in order to enjoy this sempiternal youth was to eat an apple.

He did not reach this region but rather another where the trees (the only one missing was the apple tree) grew, blossomed, gave fruit and withered in a week; where the ladies (always young) became pregnant at night, gave birth the next morning and seven days later the children were the size of their parents, who then died.

Seeing himself surrounded by so much brief life, the knight Guingamor—whose person had suffered no change at all—felt his own time somehow expanded. He stayed there, very happy.

"Either he forgot he had been seeking the region of the long-lived, not the region of the ephemera, or in view of the circumstances it made no difference," the chronicle ends.

ORPHEUS AND EURYDICE

Orpheus remembered the warning the kings of Death had given him: "You may take Eurydice with you, brought to life

183

again; go, and Eurydice will follow you; but when you leave this subterranean kingdom of shadows you must not look back; if you do, you will lose Eurydice forever."

Then Orpheus, realizing it would be of no use to him because, by his very nature, he was not made for loving any woman, turned his head and looked over his shoulder at Eurydice.

From the depths of hell he heard, as in a distant echo, the voice of the twice-dead Eurydice. And that feminine "Good-bye" sounded with all the scorn of a terrible accusation.

ARGUS

Zeus would tell a story and all the eyes of the gods, open and attentive, would follow his every gesture. Hermes envied that great power the narrator exercised over his many-eyed audience. And so he felt happy when he was given the mission of going to entertain Argus. It was the hour of twilight. He sat down in the meadow, facing Argus, who was lifting into the air his huge hundred-eyed head, and began to tell the story of Syrinx, flattered by the illusion that a vast audience was paying attention to him. But Hermes was not Zeus, and the greatest humiliation of his life was when, one after another, the hundred eyes began closing and Argus, bored, fell asleep. Then, piqued, Hermes—creature of deeds, not words—beheaded Argus with one stroke of his sword and over the meadow there was an immense night without stars.

MYTHOLOGIES

As the head of Argus, decapitated by Hermes, went bouncing down the precipice, a strange shudder passed through the feathers of a turkey, asleep in the gardens of Hera. The turkey awoke peacock, with all the eyes of Argus set into its feathers.

The fifty daughters of Danaus suffered at first, when they were condemned to transport the water in broken jars. As some were coming out of the river with their pitchers streaming, others were returning with their pitchers already dry. Thus the way was always traveled by the double line of sisters. They suffered, but only at first; because afterward, when they went mad, the Danaides were happy: in their madness they thought they were the river.

The red-haired Galanthis brightened the countryside with her laughter and her falsehoods. She was all mouth. And through the mouth an offended goddess condemned her to give birth. From then on her children were born as characters in oral tales are born. And if the Muses wanted to have nothing to do with this Galanthis, laughing narrator, it was because they did not yet know the Novel.

It was folly for the river Achelous to challenge Heracles to combat. Greater folly still for it to take, in order to fight, the shape of a man, a serpent, a bull. Heracles always defeated it. Only at the end, when Achelous recovered its river fluidity, did Heracles begin to seek it out, swimming in the waves of water, and at not finding it he declared himself beaten.

Someone feels sorry for Sisyphus on seeing that with both hands he pushes an enormous stone to the summit and then the stone falls again, and once more he raises it, and once more it rolls to the bottom.

"Poor thing!" exclaims the pitier.

"But I'm playing!" he answers with the smile of an athletic giant.

With the tips of his fingers he picked up a speck of the ashes left by the Phoenix on its funeral pyre and tossed it to the wind. Resurging from its ashes, the Phoenix resurged incomplete, with one eye missing.

There was one vulture who refused to peck at the entrails of Prometheus. Unfortunately we know nothing about him because the contempt of the others condemned him to oblivion.

A labyrinth is a building but it is also an idea. Contravening the idea men have of a dwellingplace, Daedalus constructed his labyrinth, which came to be an upside-down idea. There he set loose the Minotaur; but the Minotaur roamed through the corridors of the building, not the corridors of the idea. That huge bull head could not know it was in a labyrinth.

Orpheus descended into Hades to visit the dead. It was a large place, with its sky full of stars, with seas, mountains, woods, plains, cities, gardens and cemeteries. He spoke with the dead. They never considered him a visitor. They did not even know they were dead.

How the bark of Charon was able to leave the Styx and climb so high I do not know: but there it was, sailing over the mountain, in the vast twilight sky.

The Sphinx used to punish those who gave wrong answers to her questions. Those who knew enough to say "I don't know" went on their way, safe and sound.

King Erysichthon, castigated by Demeter with an irrepressible voracity, sold all he had in order to eat and eat and eat. At last all he had left was a daughter, whom he also decided to sell. As the girl had received from Poseidon the gift of changing shape and could turn herself into cow, mare, rabbit or hen, Erysichthon thought of selling her to Proteus.

It stopped raining. A rainbow was trembling on a leaf. Euterpe picked the leaf and, pointing out the raindrop, said to Polyhymnia:
"Do you see what I see? The siren Aglaophania sings, Poseidon waves his trident, Aphrodite comes forth. . . ."

Atlas was standing, his legs well apart, bearing the world on his shoulders. Hyperion asked him:
"I suppose, Atlas, it's heavier for you every time an aerolite falls and is embedded in the earth."
"Exactly," Atlas replied. "And, on the contrary, sometimes I feel lightened when a bird takes flight."

The nine Muses punished those nine women, daughters of Pierus, who had insolently challenged them to a literary contest. They punished them by turning them into chattering magpies. The Muses could not prevent, however, the fact that many artists prefer to be inspired by the Pierides. One must understand those artists. After all, the Muses lived very much exalted; and the Pierides, in contrast, who were like shadows of the Muses, lived bound to the earth and their language seemed more realistic to them.

STARBIRTH

BY ALBERT GOLDBARTH

How headlights sugar
the lot's last abandoned shopping cart,
and a new constellation
hangs low in the evening obscurity: The
Cage. All the fingerprints
fondled onto its surface
whorl in the distance like galaxies. This
is the night for it, this is the explanation
of what armed paladin or winged firebreathing
poodle was kenneled long ago, this
is the spangled ascension of new constellations,
The Rock Star's Glitter, her stage dress flung
backstage and the ancient story told in moaning
while a dropped match picks off glints
on celestial shoulderstraps. This is
the tragic lightings of everyone's life, The Proctoscopy
in appropriate magnitude, Ambulance Flasher,
The Arsonist's Spark. How the littlest wonders
belong in solar commemoration: Cat Eyes
Filled With A Trucker's Brights; Amino Acids
In Nova. Now
what's lactal, or citric, or transistorized, wants its
own black velvet. Now everything you see
could torch its ganglia
and lift
off the planet, and burn only what's most
essential for identification: The Chess Master's Brain
like a phone's gut. Now
the wind drops, now on the endless horizon

your body goes blank
as a night sky, now
the myths
in your nervous system are rising.

NOTES ON THE CONTRIBUTORS

ENRIQUE ANDERSON IMBERT was born in Argentina in 1910 and came to the United States in 1947 to teach at the University of Michigan. He is now at Harvard in a professorship created especially for him. Two of his thirty books have appeared in English: *Fugue* and *The Other Side of the Mirror.*

MICHAEL BISHOP's novella *On the Street of the Serpents* was a Nebula Award finalist in 1975. His second novel, *And Strange at Ecbatan the Trees,* has recently been published by Harper & Row, and a third novel, *Stolen Faces,* is due to appear (again, from Harper & Row) shortly. He lives in Georgia with his wife and children.

MICHAEL CONNER was a student at Clarion Science Fiction Workshop in 1974. "Extinction of Confidence, the Exercise of Honesty" is his first published story. He is a native of Minneapolis.

JACK DANN has taught science fiction at Cornell University and Broome Community College. His first sf anthology, *Wandering Stars,* was published in 1974 by Harper & Row, as was *Faster Than Light* (co-editor, George Zebrowski). His novella *Junction* was a Nebula Award finalist in 1973. He lives and works in upstate New York.

DAVID DIEFENDORF writes poetry and fiction and is an editor at the Columbia University Press.

THOMAS M. DISCH is on page 238 of Braudel's *The Mediterranean and the Mediterranean World in the Age of Philip II* (Vol. I) and watches "Mary Hartman, Mary Hartman" faithfully.

JON FAST was born in New York City in 1948, attended the High School of Music and Art, Princeton, Sarah Lawrence, and did graduate work at the University of California (Berkeley). His short fiction has appeared in *F & SF* and *Last Dangerous Visions.*

ALBERT GOLDBARTH was a National Book Award nominee in 1975 for his collection of poems *Jan 31.* His new collection, *Comings Back,* will be published by Doubleday this year. He lives in Ithaca, where it rains.

WINN KEARNS is divorced and lives in Portland, Oregon. She has a degree in journalism from Northwestern University and at one time called square dances at a North Carolina craft school.

R. A. LAFFERTY is no stranger to sf readers. In a recent letter he writes of the genre: "The once likeable strumpet named SF has become a vile and rotting old harridan of dishonest attitude, a change brought about by both young and old practitioners who say that they want her that way."

RHODA LERMAN calls herself an "unemployed astronaut" and lives with her husband and three children in the Syracuse area. Her second novel, *The Girl That He Marries,* was published in June by Holt, Rinehart & Winston.

HARRY MARTINSON was born in Sweden in 1904 and went to sea when he was fifteen. His epic science-fiction poem *Aniara* was adapted for use as an opera libretto, several sections of which were used in Kubrick/Clarke's film *2001.* He was awarded the Nobel Prize for Literature in 1974.

JERROLD J. MUNDIS's newest novel, *Gerhardt's Children,* will be published in 1976 by Atheneum. He lives in upstate New York with his wife and two sons.

CHARLES NAYLOR, coeditor, has stories in both *Bad Moon Rising* and *The New Improved Sun,* and has published several novels pseudonymously. He lives in New York City.

KATHRYN PAULSEN is editor of *The Woman's Almanac* and is currently working on her second novel.

ROBERT SHECKLEY has written many science-fiction novels and stories. A resident of the island of Ibiza for many years, he has recently resettled in London with his wife and infant daughter.

JOHN SLADEK lives in London but was born in Minnesota. He has published several novels and stories and *The New Apocrypha,* a guide to strange sciences and occult beliefs.

BEEBE THARP has written some short fiction but is better known for her essays and lectures on pre-Renaissance music. "The Harp That Conquered Hell" is her first published science-fiction story.

GENE WOLFE, in his own words, is "younger than Michael Bishop but older than R. A. Lafferty." His first novel, *Peace,* was published in 1975 by Harper & Row.

GEORGE ZEBROWSKI's stories have appeared in *Amazing, F & SF,* and other magazines. His novels include *The Omega Point* and *Star Web.* From 1970 until 1975 he co-edited the SFWA bulletin with Jack Dann.